The Impact of Organisational Culture on Knowledge Management

CHANDOS
KNOWLEDGE MANAGEMENT SERIES

Series Editor: Melinda Taylor
(email: melindataylor@chandospublishing.com)

Chandos' new series of books are aimed at all those individuals interested in knowledge management. They have been specially commissioned to provide the reader with an authoritative view of current thinking. If you would like a full listing of current and forthcoming titles, please visit our web site **www.chandospublishing.com** or contact Hannah Grace-Williams on email info@chandospublishing.com or telephone number +44 (0) 1865 884447.

New authors: we are always pleased to receive ideas for new titles; if you would like to write a book for Chandos, please contact Dr Glyn Jones on email gjones@chandospublishing.com or telephone number +44 (0) 1865 884447.

Bulk orders: some organisations buy a number of copies of our books. If you are interested in doing this, we would be pleased to discuss a discount. Please contact Hannah Grace-Williams on email info@chandospublishing.com or telephone number +44 (0) 1865 884447.

The Impact of Organisational Culture on Knowledge Management

MARINA DU PLESSIS

Chandos Publishing

Oxford · England

Chandos Publishing (Oxford) Limited
Chandos House
5 & 6 Steadys Lane
Stanton Harcourt
Oxford OX29 5RL
UK
Tel: +44 (0) 1865 884447 Fax: +44 (0) 1865 884448
Email: info@chandospublishing.com
www.chandospublishing.com

First published in Great Britain in 2006

ISBN:
1 84334 295 2 (paperback)
1 84334 296 0 (hardback)
978 1 84334 295 3 (paperback)
978 1 84334 296 0 (hardback)

© M. du Plessis, 2006

Typeset by Domex e-Data Pvt. Ltd.
Printed in the UK and USA.

Printed in the UK by 4edge Limited - www.4edge.co.uk

Contents

List of figures

About the author

Dr du Plessis started her career as a management consultant at Coopers and Lybrand in Pretoria, South Africa, where she worked for two years. Thereafter she joined the management consulting practice of Price Waterhouse in Johannesburg. It was here where she became involved in knowledge management for four years. She spent 6 months of her career in the London and Dallas offices of PricewaterhouseCoopers (by then, the two companies had merged) where she worked in their knowledge management centre of excellence and assisted in the roll-out of their new global knowledge portal. She returned to South Africa to set up a centre of excellence for the South African practice, which was eventually used by the offices in Zimbabwe and Namibia. It also served countries such as the USA, UK, Asia, the Middle East and Australia on an ad hoc basis.

Dr du Plessis then joined a South African strategic management consulting company, Bentley West Management Consultants, where she also set up a knowledge management centre of excellence in conjunction with a black empowerment company that they were partnering with.

Subsequently Dr du Plessis became Head of Knowledge Management at Absa, one of the largest retail banks in South Africa. She defined a strategy and implementation plan which was spearheaded by a number of communities of practice which were implemented successfully. The knowledge management strategy was also integrated with other highly strategic initiatives in the bank.

Currently, Dr. du Plessis works as an independent business advisor in the field of knowledge management and business strategy.

Dr du Plessis has authored a number of articles in the International Journal of Information Management, and some of her articles on knowledge management are due to be published in the Journal of Knowledge Management in 2007.

Dr du Plessis obtained her PhD in Information Science from the University of Pretoria, South Africa, in 2003 under the auspices of Prof. Hans Boon. The title of her thesis was 'The role of knowledge management in customer relationship management and eBusiness'.

If you would like to contact Dr du Plessis, please feel free to do so. Her contact details are:

Email: *marinaduplessis@hotmail.com* or
      marinaduplessis@discoverymail.co.za
Postal address: PO Box 15747
                Lyttelton
                0140
                South Africa
Mobile number: +27 82 4520479

Introduction

Every organisation has a unique organisational culture. This is due to the fact that unique individuals work in these organisations and make up the unique culture of that particular organisation. This brings a wonderful sense of uniqueness to our world, making it exciting and different everywhere we go. But it also poses unique challenges, as no two organisations' cultures are ever the same. Due to the fact that all organisational cultures differ, a number of programmes in the organisations are also uniquely impacted, such as knowledge management.

Organisational culture has a huge impact on organisational programmes such as knowledge management programmes. This impact can be either positive or negative. The impact is, however, so great that it makes it impossible to have a blueprint for implementing knowledge management across all organisations. Each implementation will be different due to the differences posed by the unique organisational cultures. This is also true for the different elements of the programme, including strategy, technology, measurement, processes, structuring, value and other personal related issues. This makes knowledge management implementations extremely complex, especially in the planning and design phases, as the knowledge management team will have very little information on what will work and what won't, except what they know from experience.

Their knowledge management journey will largely be made up of learning through experience as they go along, through trial and error.

The challenge for knowledge management practitioners is to understand what the particular organisational cultural issues in their organisations are and to be able to address them, in order for the organisational culture to impact the knowledge management programme of the organisation positively. Whilst it is not always possible to change an entire organisation's corporate culture, the second step is to work on the organisation's knowledge management culture to try and influence that as much as possible by being aware of how the organisational culture is impacting the knowledge management culture in a positive or negative manner, and by trying to make the knowledge management programme run as effectively as possible within the given organisational culture.

Of course this sounds like an easy thing to do, whilst in reality it is probably one of the most complex things to do.

| Figure 1 | Unique organisational cultures impact knowledge management programmes |

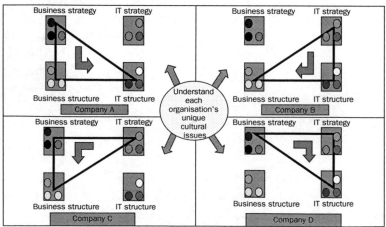

There is no blueprint for mapping organisational culture to knowledge management culture, and therefore many organisations have a hard time understanding this complex subject.

Culture is often the ability to self-organise in chaos (Stahle, 2000, p.41). It is a concept that underlies many other things and is not always very identifiable per se, and therefore the subject matter is very complex (see Figure 1).

Definition of a knowledge management culture

Prior to defining knowledge management culture, knowledge management as concept should be defined. Knowledge management is a planned, structured approach to manage the creation, sharing, harvesting and leveraging of knowledge as an organisational asset, to enhance an organisation's ability, speed and effectiveness in delivering products or services for the benefit of clients, in line with its business strategy. Knowledge management takes place on three levels, namely the individual level, team level and organisational level. It is a holistic solution incorporating a variety of perspectives, namely people, process, culture and technology perspectives, all of which carry equal weighting in managing knowledge (Du Plessis & Boon, 2004).

Secondly, culture needs to be defined. The culture of an organisation is an amalgamation of the values and beliefs of the people in an organisation. It can be felt in the implicit rules and expectations of behaviour in an organisation where, even though the rules may not be formally written down, employees know what is expected of them. It is usually set by the management team whose decisions on policies and procedures influence the culture of the organisation. The organisational culture usually has values and beliefs that support the organisational goals and objectives, and is pervasive throughout the organisation.

Organisational culture is also complex in the fact that it can differ in different areas of the organisation. For example, in large organisations, each department may have a different culture. There may therefore be an organisational culture as well as departmental culture. There may even be more hidden cultures. If the organisation is sophisticated enough to have communities of practice, there may be a culture formed within these larger communities of specialists as well. There are therefore a number of cultures to be aware of in an organisation that can impact on the knowledge management programme. Some may be more subtle than others, but it is important for the knowledge management programme to identify these cultures and subcultures to understand what the impact is or may be, and how to deal with it.

Knowledge management culture is defined as making knowledge sharing the norm in an organisation. To create a knowledge sharing culture the organisation needs to encourage people to work together more effectively, to collaborate and to share – ultimately to make organisational knowledge more productive.

The purpose of knowledge sharing is to help an organisation as a whole to meet its business objectives. Changing a culture is difficult. Not only does it mean change – which has always been difficult – it means seeing the world in a different way. Some define a knowledge management culture as a perpetually changing common knowledge and shared meaning.

In fact, the question begs whether a knowledge management culture can ever be defined, as it is so unique to each and every organisation. It is based on the knowledge management needs and behaviours of the individuals in the organisation, and their dynamics in teams when working in the knowledge management lifecycle that determines the knowledge management culture of an organisational culture. Therefore it is so unique that it is virtually impossible for it to be similar from one organisation to the next.

The values of an organisation play a large part in creating the knowledge management culture. If an organisation has the values of transparency and trust, knowledge sharing will take place more readily. If an organisation does not have a knowledge creating and knowledge sharing culture, it is a very difficult and slow process to bring about change, due to the fact that the organisation's and people's values have to change first to create such a knowledge creating and sharing culture, and this is usually quite a slow process in itself. Values are inherent in individuals, and therefore inherently change slowly.

The cultural issues around knowledge management are very important to the organisation. A specific environment needs to be created to foster knowledge management. When creating new knowledge, for example, old thought patterns must be broken. Intuition and innovation should be encouraged in a knowledge management environment. Chaos is an imperative precondition for a new perspective or mindset. Knowledge management is aimed at learning to understand the nature of the chaos, and to create methods, practices and culture that utilise the ability of chaos to self-organise. This, in most cases, goes against the much organised environment of the corporate world we work in. In most organisations we strive to create structure and rigor and rules by which we work, which is not a very conducive environment for the creation of knowledge and the free flow of knowledge.

This antithesis is what is causing many knowledge management implementations to fail. The way organisations are set up today is in a way that contradicts the rules that make knowledge management programmes successful. The cultures created by organisations today challenges knowledge management programmes to come up with innovative ways of working to ensure that these challenges are identified and met, to ensure that knowledge management can be implemented successfully, and especially that knowledge management cultures enhance organisational cultures.

Many organisations think of knowledge management as a technical programme with the typical plan of a strategy, structure, processes and measures, but often forget the very powerful element of culture in implementation of knowledge management. Of all these elements in knowledge management, culture is most probably the element with the biggest impact in implementation, but the one with the least visibility. It is difficult to recognise the cultural elements that are causing issues or problems in a knowledge management implementation and therefore the failure rate of implementations are high.

The purpose of this book is to highlight some organisational culture issues that can either positively or negatively impact knowledge management programmes. The aim is to make it easier for knowledge management practitioners to identify these areas, and to enable them to address them earlier and in a more effective way than before.

3

Business areas impacting on knowledge management culture

The organisational culture impacts knowledge management in various areas. Knowledge management is impacted by people issues, technology and other channel issues, process issues, measurement issues, strategy and leadership issues, organisational structure issues and other operational issues. In order to successfully design and implement a knowledge management programme, it is of crucial importance to understand these issues and how they interrelate with one another and with the rest of the organisation. The issues and how they relate to each other are not always as clear as they seem, and can create havoc in the design and implementation of knowledge management.

People related issues

Employees do not understand the value proposition of knowledge management

Employees often attach importance to strategic knowledge to ensure innovation and a competitive edge. Knowledge management does not play or seem to play a significant part in the strategic decision-making process. Employees thus understand the strategic importance of knowledge and knowledge management, but only apply knowledge and knowledge management on an operational level (Du Plessis, 2003; GartnerGroup, 2000; KPMG Consulting, 2000; PricewaterhouseCoopers, 1999, pp. 1–2; Zyngier, 2006). This is supported by the fact that knowledge management is not integrated into the business, e.g. into the business process value chain, but is mostly implemented as an administrative function. Organisations face two unique challenges to overcome this. The first challenge is to extract maximum value from knowledge and knowledge management on a strategic level. To enable these organisations to extract the value from knowledge management, they firstly need to understand the value that knowledge and knowledge management can provide on a strategic level. These organisations need to appoint leaders to drive knowledge management from a strategic platform, ensuring that it is tied to the business strategy and supports strategic decision-making and adaptation to changes in the marketplace. The knowledge management sponsor should also link the strategic and operational application of knowledge and knowledge management by linking knowledge to the business process value chain of the organisation, which in turn assists in execution of the business strategy, but also ties into the operational part of the business. Through the linkage of knowledge and knowledge management to the organisational value chain, knowledge and knowledge management will be embedded in the day-to-day activities of employees, allowing knowledge management to become an integral part of the organisation (Du Plessis & Boon, 2004).

Knowledge management allows collaboration

Knowledge management facilitates a collaborative working culture through the provision of collaboration tools, collaboration environments and the encouragement of collaboration values (Mudge, 1999; Van der Kamp, 2001).

Good organisation and access to all knowledge assets will stimulate more collaboration in more communities, and the quality of the collaboration will be improved as well. Knowledge management increases collaboration through the provision of appropriate technology, as well as forums, e.g. communities of practice. Knowledge management also ensures that processes and platforms exist to convert tacit knowledge to explicit knowledge within knowledge exchanges in virtual communities or collaborative forums. Value can thus be extracted from tacit knowledge, and knowledge attrition can be minimised. The insight and knowledge shared in a collaborative effort will also improve as employees are given the ability to identify experts to resolve issues.

In the eBusiness environment, collaboration is becoming increasingly prevalent. eBusinesses collaboratively design products across geographical boundaries and sometimes across organisational boundaries. There is also collaboration in the form of virtual communities internal and external to the organisation, e.g. through intranets and extranets. These communities share knowledge on a wide variety of issues. Knowledge management provides the technology, processes and platforms to enable the said collaboration. Knowledge management also ensures the retention and structuring of the knowledge shared in these collaborative forums that can be used as input to further knowledge creation within these and other forums. Due to collaborative design taking place across geographical and organisational boundaries through provision of collaboration forums and related knowledge management tools and processes, the organisation's time to market decreases and agility increases (Havens & Knapp, 1999; Kennedy, 1996; KPMG, 2000; O' Dell & Grayson, 1999).

In the customer relationship management environment collaboration is becoming increasingly prevalent due to organisations expanding their reach and working across geographical boundaries. The knowledge harvested and shared in collaborative customer forums are used to build customer profiles, and is used as business intelligence to do market, customer, as well as product and service segmentation and marketing.

All of this creates an innovative culture in the organisation where people feel that they are at the forefront of new developments. Knowledge management therefore directly impacts the organisational culture by driving it to be a new economy culture.

Knowledge management improves communication in the organisation

Communication of knowledge can also be clearer due to the knowledge management programme providing of platforms for communication, whether in tacit or explicit format (GartnerGroup, 2000; Mudge, 1999; Temkin, 2001).

Communication with suppliers and business partners is a critical component of any organisation's ability to develop, produce, and deliver products or services. Knowledge management plays a role in facilitating communication through the provision of technology, processes and platforms that enables communication. These technologies, processes and platforms are especially useful in organisations with diverse geographical locations and associated timezones, as well as in cases where there are functional silos in the organisation that hamper communication and knowledge flow. Knowledge management also ensures the retention of customer knowledge shared in these communication forums for future use (Havens & Knapp, 1999; KPMG, 2000).

Knowledge management plays a role in facilitating communication through the provision of technology, processes and platforms that enable communication. These technologies, processes and platforms are especially useful in the eBusinesses world, with diverse geographical locations and associated timezones, or where organisational silos are present that inhibit communication and knowledge sharing. Knowledge management also ensures the retention of knowledge shared in these communication forums for future use. Because communication is faster and more flexible than before, organisations have the opportunity to sit down with their business partners and redesign business processes across organisations to realise joint gains.

A culture of communication can therefore be instilled in the organisation using knowledge management as a vehicle. It allows for quick, easy and up-to-date communication in the organisation that is easily accessible to all employees.

The impact of a lack of understanding of skills and knowledge available in the organisation

An organisation's culture can be such that it does not take stock of the skills, abilities and knowledge that it has. These skills, abilities and knowledge are resources of the organisation that can be used to improve the efficiency of the organisation in numerous ways. There is, in most cases, however, no way or mechanism to know what skills, abilities or knowledge exist.

Organisations should strive to create platforms to enable staff members to understand what skills, abilities and knowledge are available to assist them in their daily work environment. These can take multiple forms, some examples being yellow pages with listed skills per staff member, an intranet with communities of practice where knowledge is shared, or a skills database where staff members' core skills are listed. This will enable people to identify and use knowledge as a resource in their daily work environments. In most instances, they do not use it because they simply do not know that it exists.

The impact of language barriers

Having multiple languages spoken in an organisation can be a challenge for implementing knowledge management. Some organisations have a dominant business language that they use, e.g. English, and most employees are proficient enough in English to be able to share their knowledge in English. This is not the case everywhere, however. A lot of multi-nationals have problems being able to share knowledge on, e.g. manufacturing processes, in countries across the world, e.g. Russia, Hungary, Peru, Mexico, Uganda, Lesotho. Sometimes they have to deal with staff who speak 20 to 30 different languages, who are not proficient in English, across their organisations globally. South Africa, for example, has 11 official languages and some European languages are also spoken, which may render knowledge management a concept that is more difficult to implement compared to countries such as the UK where one language is dominant. South African organisations are therefore faced with many unique challenges relating to the country-specific conditions with reference to the number of languages, and can therefore not necessarily follow the American or European models of knowledge management implementations.

Organisations must take language differences into account when designing and implementing knowledge management programmes (Merali, 2000, p. 83). Once again, this will differ from organisation to organisation and by nature makes knowledge management programmes very unique to each particular organisation.

Language is, of course, very closely tied to a country and individual's culture, and therefore the language(s) that the organisation use will have a huge impact on the success on the knowledge management programme. Sharing of knowledge is very difficult to do in a second or third language if one is not proficient in it, and a lot of the context may be lost. This may impair the knowledge sharing process. Language is also closely linked to culture and the link between language and knowledge management needs to be explored further.

The impact of differing levels of literacy issues

Another knowledge management cultural element that needs consideration is literacy of the population in the country and the organisation.

There is a high level of limited knowledge management literacy in countries such as Zimbabwe and South Africa. This means that knowledge management programmes will differ from those countries like the US and UK, where there are high levels of knowledge management literacy. Examples may be in using touch-screen knowledge management systems with graphic images denoting specific knowledge nuggets or activities, which may be easier to use for people with limited literacy than text based systems. This may be especially applicable in certain industries e.g. mining, manufacturing, environmental management, conservation, etc. In South Africa, for example, illiterate wildlife conservationists use electronic hand held devices with the pictures of the tracks of animals to gather data on the movement of wildlife in wilderness parks. This is a good example of knowledge management being used without necessarily using a traditional personal computer.

In a highly sophisticated environment, only the latest technology will be accepted by users to share knowledge, which means that a needs assessment should be undertaken to ascertain what type of knowledge management programme will foster and grow in a particular culture prior to implementation. This will ensure that the knowledge management programme that is implemented is adaptable to the environment and the people using it, in order for the user adoption to be high.

Co-creation of knowledge management solutions allows easier user adoption

When embarking on a knowledge management implementation, organisations usually have a knowledge management team that is tasked to do the design and implementation of the programme. One of the weaknesses such a team may have is working in isolation, and not interacting with the business enough. Co-creation of knowledge management solutions plays an important role in the acceptance of the knowledge management solutions in the organisation. It is important for the knowledge management division or team to design knowledge management solutions with inputs from people in the business. Business has very particular knowledge management needs that the knowledge management design team often does not know of, and will miss if they do not engage the staff to determine their requirements.

It is imperative to take the business on the journey with the team. The team needs to understand the issues that the organisation is faced with day to day, how they currently try to overcome it, and what potential solutions they foresee. A strategy with a vision, mission, goal, objectives, critical success factors, measures of success, risks, costs, benefits, etc. needs to be developed in conjunction with business in order to ensure that the knowledge management team understands the environment and its issues, but also to ensure that the business buys into the process and individuals feel that they are being heard and this is not a solution that will be forced onto them, but actually something that will address their needs as identified and formulated by themselves in conjunction with the knowledge management team.

This will also ensure quicker user adoption at the implementation stage and training stage, as people will already have an understanding of what the programme is really about.

An example is to create an implementation community of practice for knowledge management, where members of the implementation team shares knowledge with people from other parts of the organisation such as Human Resources, Strategy, Finance, Technology and Strategic Business Units. In this way, everyone can give their input, and they also know what input will be required from them to make the programme a success.

It also ensures agreements between parties are recorded in minutes, so that rework is prevented and that everyone knows where they are in the design and implementation process. This is a very positive step to ensure that knowledge management is implemented quickly and efficiently. It records the design, build and implementation process properly for all parties to see.

Without a culture of co-creation, buy-in to the knowledge management programme will be very difficult to obtain. The organisation will experience knowledge management as just another initiative being forced upon them, in which they have to take part. Uptake will be slow, and the resistance factor will be high. It will take some time to break these barriers down and resistance will persist.

With a culture of co-creation, buy-in and user acceptance for knowledge management solutions is ensured, as the users are part of the design from the start and their ideas and knowledge are incorporated into the building of the end solutions. This makes for much quicker uptake of the solution, less marketing expenditure and effort, and less communication that needs to be done. Even training is easier, as users understand the concepts behind the knowledge management solutions are not new.

From a strategic perspective it also breaks down silo behaviour and encourages knowledge sharing from the start. People from different parts of the organisation are brought together to design knowledge management solutions together, and in such a way that they get to know more about each others needs as well as each others' working environments. This helps later in the programme to provide mind maps of the organisation with respect to how knowledge flows and the value of how it is done. It also provides an understanding of how the organisational structure fits together.

Co-creation of solutions is really the first step in creating a knowledge-rich culture in the organisation, and it is essential if one wants to entrench the culture into the organisation's strategy and processes (see Figure 1).

Understanding the impact of knowledge management roles and responsibilities

Every knowledge management programme has roles and responsibilities associated with it, not only for those people who manage the programme but also for all the employees in the organisation. To enable knowledge management to be implemented and entrenched into the culture of the organisation, it is imperative that every person is absolutely clear on what their roles and responsibilities are with respect to knowledge management. Unless this happens, a knowledge management culture will never be instilled in an organisation.

The knowledge management leadership team should ensure that staff in the organisation are trained on what their roles and responsibilities are with respect to knowledge management and that they receive refresher training every year. Staff should be measured on whether they attend the training and also on whether they actually participated in the knowledge management activities, i.e. whether learning did take place.

Job and role profiles have to be defined for the knowledge management implementation and management team by Human Resources, so that staff are well aware of what their duties are and what their roles and responsibilities are. There should be no ambiguity on this front. It is also important that members of staff understand what the knowledge management team's responsibilities are to ensure successful implementation. Often implementations fail due to senior members of staff using knowledge management staff for other projects or other pieces of work, which means that the knowledge management is never completed, or a lag factor sets in.

Group dynamics differ with respect to the human response to change, pace and vision regarding knowledge management

Knowledge management is different in each organisation, due to the fact that it is so interwoven with the culture of the organisation. There can never be a blueprint for implementation for knowledge management because of this fact.

When group dynamics are investigated, one can look at groups within the organisation, but also the organisation as one entire group. If one deals with groups within the organisation, e.g. communities of practice, it is extremely important to understand that each of these knowledge sharing and knowledge creation groups have their own goals, their own vision, and their own way of working. They also have their own pace of working and sharing knowledge, i.e. they have their own unique culture within the organisational culture. All these different groups' dynamics will differ and that is very important to understand from a management point of view, when trying to manage a knowledge management programme from a cultural point of view. Different groups will have different dynamics in creating, sharing, harvesting and leveraging their knowledge.

Once again, there is no blueprint that one can use to set up these communities of practice. Guidelines can be provided, but the community members themselves have to decide how they would like to operate within their community, and how they are going to create, share, harvest and leverage knowledge in that particular community. This uniqueness must be encouraged, or else the knowledge management culture will not thrive in the organisation. Knowledge management is not something that the organisation can be too prescriptive about from a cultural point of view.

Appreciation of diverse perspectives can lead to limited knowledge sharing

The human being and the human psyche are different in each of us and we all see things differently. This is also true with respect to the way we see knowledge management and the value it adds to our lives, and to the lives of others.

Knowledge is often only shared by a person if it directly impacts that person's environment. This means that a lot of very important knowledge in an organisation is not shared explicitly, but only tacitly, due to the narrow focus on just what is important to the person in question. Knowledge is often not shared for the 'greater good' of the organisation to other areas where it may be very useful. Thus, a silo approach is often created independent from organisational structure but by means of the working world of the individual, which is compounded when one adds a number of individuals working as a team in one area together.

The fact that people also have very diverse opinions on topics of knowledge in an organisation can lead to very diverse perspectives. Some people are prepared to share their diverse perspectives on various areas of knowledge, whilst others may have more introverted personalities and hence choose not share their diverse perspectives. They choose to keep their knowledge in tacit format. Unless the organisation has a means to extract that knowledge into an explicit format, or has a way to utilise it in its tacit state, it may be lost to the organisation.

A diversity of perspectives in the organisation is therefore a good sign of innovativeness and knowledge creation. The ability to exert leverage to extract the knowledge is where the organisation needs to be clever, as this is where the knowledge can be lost.

'Knowledge is power' mindset

Knowledge hoarding takes place due to the 'knowledge is power' syndrome that exists in many organisations (Zyngier, 2006). Hoarding often also takes place within functional silos in the organisation, especially where competition exists between various areas of the business. There is very little inter-organisational knowledge flow between different divisions or areas in the organisation. Knowledge management can assist in overcoming this barrier through rewarding people for sharing their knowledge. People also often hoard knowledge because no proper platforms exist to enable them to share their knowledge effectively. Knowledge management can provide these knowledge-sharing platforms, not only through technology (intranets, databases, etc.), but also through other concepts such as communities of practice and communities of interest.

The 'knowledge is power' culture also differs in different parts of the world. In the developed world knowledge is shared more freely and openly, whilst in the developing world knowledge is hoarded to a greater extent. This may be due to the oversupply of labour in some of the countries in the developing world, where the labour market is fiercely competitive. Knowledge, skills and experience are what sets an individual apart from another and ensures that they can obtain a position in an organisation and retain it. In the developed world, knowledge is shared more freely and openly as the feeling is that knowledge sharing builds a person's reputation as a specialist in a specific area.

This mindset is one of the most difficult cultural issues to address in the knowledge management environment. Unless an organisation has procedures in place to translate tacit knowledge to explicit knowledge and unless it has some reward and/or recognition system in place, it will be very difficult to turn the organisation around into one with a knowledge sharing culture (Snowden, 2000, p.9). Ultimately, knowledge is vested in individuals, and unless individuals can be persuaded to part with their knowledge it just won't happen (Gordon & Smith, 2006). Therefore recognition and reward is imperative (see Figure 2).

Figure 2	The 'knowledge is power' mindset negatively impacts the knowledge management lifecycle

The knowledge is power mindset is often caused by a lack of
knowledge sharing platforms as well as processes and procedures

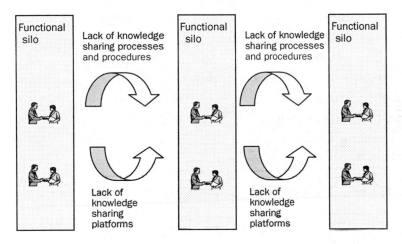

Power games lead to lack of knowledge sharing

Sometimes knowledge does not flow well between the different levels in a hierarchical organisation. People in management positions or higher positions in the organisation are often not open to sharing their skills, abilities and knowledge with people at lower levels in the hierarchy. This ties in with the 'knowledge is power' phenomenon, but is much more difficult to detect and to address.

The reason for the hesitance in sharing knowledge is that, with the phenomenal growth rate of knowledge, older people may feel threatened by the new economy knowledge that younger people bring to the organisation. They therefore hold on to their practical experience, which is something tacit and difficult to copy, and therefore difficult to replace. It is also something that younger people will not have due to their age and the shorter time they have spent in the job market.

This can be very detrimental to the organisation as a wealth of valuable knowledge can be lost to the organisation through older, experienced people not sharing their knowledge. This is especially true when they leave the organisation or when they go on to retirement (Gordon & Smith, 2006). Some organisations have programmes in place where people are given the task of sitting with some of these potential retirees to tap their knowledge a year or two ahead of their retirement, to ensure that their knowledge is not lost to the organisation. This has turned out to be a very valuable activity for these organisations.

Time to share knowledge

In today's highly-pressurised work environment, people complain that they don't have time to do knowledge management. They do not have time to capture lessons learnt on databases, they do not have time to capture best practices on databases in order for other staff members to draw from their experiences – there simply isn't time to do any of this (Hall, 2006, p.4).

In this highly-pressurised environment, one of two things can happen in an organisation. The first is that the organisation can fall into the rut of not sharing knowledge at all, due to staff members being too busy with their daily tasks in order to participate in formal knowledge management activities. This has a negative impact on the organisation as valuable learning opportunity is lost and cannot be regained. It is, however, clear that very few organisations actually set aside time during the working day with the specific purpose to share knowledge between colleagues. This is true even in knowledge-based businesses such as management consultancies. People have not yet shifted their mindsets to new economy thinking where knowledge is seen as one of the most important resources of the organisation, and a culture is fostered where it is nurtured and grown. Until that is done, it will be very hard to create an organisation with a knowledge management culture.

Examples of organisations that have overcome this barrier are organisations that have, for example, set up Friday breakfast presentation sessions to share knowledge-sharing sessions to share what work was being performed by the organisation at client sites. Other sharing examples are updates through newsletters, e-mails, intranets, and communities of practice.

The second is that even more knowledge than ever is shared, but this knowledge is in *tacit* format. It therefore moves under the radar, is not seen explicitly and its presence and value is not seen or felt by the organisation in an explicit way. This also means that the organisational knowledge base will become more complex, because there will be more and more tacit knowledge being generated that will have to be managed. This happens in many organisations and has a snowball effect, which later makes it extremely difficult to start managing the knowledge in an explicit format.

It is therefore advisable to take time out to share knowledge in some sort of formalised way to ensure that knowledge in the corporate memory is not lost and that it is in an explicit format. It renders it more useful to the organisation as people know that it is there, where they can find it, and what value it can add.

Inadequate face to face knowledge sharing takes place in organisations today

In today's society, a lot of knowledge sharing takes place via technologies such as the telephone, videoconferencing, intranets, and e-mail. Many people feel that there are not enough face to face meetings where people get a chance to share knowledge on a one-on-one basis with their colleagues. People feel that tacit knowledge sharing through face to face contact is a valuable means of creating and sharing knowledge, but that the means for doing so are not always provided to them in the organisation.

The organisational culture can see people meeting and talking as 'wasting time', and not as a value-adding knowledge management activity. It is, however, often the start of a cycle of innovative thinking where great ideas are born and should therefore be encouraged.

Some organisations do encourage such face to face contact by creating spaces in the work environment where people can meet informally during the working day to share knowledge, such as coffee areas and chill-out (relaxation) rooms. These facilities facilitate and foster discussions about work and other subjects and are found useful by employees to share knowledge informally in a tacit format, without any formalisation. It creates an innovative environment where knowledge can be shared freely.

An individual focus with respect to ownership of knowledge prevails

Most organisations own the intellectual capital of the work that is done in the organisation. However, it seems that the organisational culture often places a lot of emphasis on who 'owns' a specific piece of intellectual capital. In many organisations, the ownership of a piece of intellectual capital is tied to an individual. Although an individual creates knowledge, it is still created within the organisation and on behalf of the organisation, and therefore belongs to the organisation.

The reluctance of people to share knowledge because they created it in an organisational context will definitely be problematic in trying to implement a knowledge management culture, as sharing knowledge will not come naturally. People will be reluctant to share knowledge unless they are recognised and rewarded for it. Measurement of participation in knowledge management will also be imperative to incentivise these individuals to participate in the knowledge management programme.

The organisational culture should inform the knowledge management culture that knowledge belongs to the organisation and is there for everyone to share and build on, in order to create an innovative and competitive environment. Knowledge is a shared resource and is not the domain of selected individuals who have certain rights pertaining to it. It is there for all to use, for the benefit of the organisation.

When faced with this issue, a knowledge manager will have to ascertain which of these factors, or combination of factors, is causing the problem in acquiring the right knowledge management skills set, to enable the mitigation of the risk. Some organisations mitigate their risk by making knowledge management training compulsory for all employees. Training should, however, be to the point, easy to understand and value adding for the attendees to ensure buy-in for the knowledge management programme in the future.

Knowledge management is yet another skill for employees to acquire

In today's working environment most people have to be highly skilled to enable them to do their jobs. Not only do they need a basic education, but also continuous education to keep them up to date in a world where the richness and reach of knowledge increases by the day. Many staff members attend additional refresher courses each year, some go back to university to study again, and some take time to read and keep in contact with movers and shakers in the industry to keep their knowledge and skills up to date. They do not want to be bothered with acquiring knowledge management skills.

Knowledge management is a relatively new concept for organisations. Staff members often feel that this is an additional skillset that they have to master. This causes negative feelings around the knowledge management programme and often the knowledge management tools are simply not used as people do not go on training and/or do not apply what they have learnt during the training courses. The training around knowledge management is not a priority for them.

This may, of course, be the result of a number of other cultural issues as well, such as lack of buy-in from senior leadership, lack of time for knowledge management, lack of recognition and rewards for knowledge management, lack of measurement of individuals' participation in the knowledge management programme, lack of understanding of the value proposition of knowledge management, or a lack of training.

A culture of 'being too busy' leads to knowledge sharing as not seen as value adding

Staff in organisations often portray a culture of 'being too busy' when it comes to knowledge creation, sharing, harvesting and leveraging. Knowledge management is not viewed as 'real work', and is therefore seen as administrative work that is not a priority in the working environment.

This culture is often created by the lack of buy-in by top management into the knowledge management programme, as well as the fact that people are not measured on whether they participate in the knowledge management programme or not, i.e. they are not rewarded or recognised for their participation. It may also be caused by a lack of understanding of the value that is added through knowledge management to the business itself. They neither understand the value for themselves nor for others in creating and sharing knowledge across the organisation, and are therefore too busy working to do this (Hall, 2006, p.4).

The culture of 'being too busy' could also be a sign of a lack of adequate training on the concept of knowledge management as such, or a lack of understanding on how some of the technology based systems work. Instead of participating in the programme, staff hide their incompetence behind a screen of being busy with other work. This often happens as knowledge management is a new economy concept and it is not always easy for people to grasp the business value thereof and the value of integrating knowledge management into their daily work environments.

Finally 'being too busy' can just be portrayed as a reason for people who do simply do not want to share their knowledge with others, and have the 'knowledge is power' syndrome. They hide behind the fact that they are always too busy to partake in knowledge sharing activities, whilst in truth they are actually withholding knowledge.

Organisational values and personal values

The values of an organisation play a large part in the knowledge management cultural issues. If an organisation has the values of transparency and trust, knowledge sharing will take place more readily. If an organisation does not have a knowledge creating and knowledge sharing culture, it is a very difficult and slow process to bring about change, due to the fact that the organisation's and people's values have to change to create such a culture (Vernon, 1999; Chait, 1999).

An organisation's values are always, however, determined by the values that individuals uphold. Values are intrinsically personal and therefore one must understand the personal dimension of knowledge management once one starts to look at values and how they impact knowledge management. The individual element can unfortunately never be taken out of the knowledge management dimension, as knowledge resides in an individual. Individuals' values will determine in what way they will create, share, harvest and leverage knowledge. Although some of the values are discussed below, there are a myriad more that have an effect in the world of knowledge management. It is important that values are seen as cornerstones of knowledge management programmes, however, because without them knowledge management processes would never be able to take place.

Trust

Trust can be defined as the firm reliance on the integrity, ability, or character of a person or thing. Trust is a necessity for knowledge sharing (Nichani, 2004). The depth and breadth of knowledge that will be shared between individuals will be determined by their levels of trust towards one another.

Once again it can be seen that not only do personal values have a huge impact on knowledge management programmes, but so do organisational values and cultures. If trust is a value considered to be an important value in the organisation, the organisation is normally found to be quite open and transparent, making the flow of knowledge easier. If, however, there is distrust e.g. between departments or areas within the business, it is likely that there will be pockets of knowledge in the organisation that will not be integrated or free-flowing due to the fact that knowledge is not shared by the individuals working in those pockets.

Values are therefore extremely important in a knowledge management programme and it all ties back to strategy and leadership. Leaders are the people who are in the position to make or break knowledge management programmes by instilling the appropriate values in the organisation that will foster the values that is necessary for knowledge management to flourish. Leaders are the people that lay the foundation of values, like trust, that filter down to the staff in the organisation and are necessary for programmes such as knowledge management to be successful (see Figure 3).

Respect

Individuals and groups in the organisation must have respect for each other's knowledge, skills and abilities to enable a knowledge management programme to be successful. This goes hand in hand with trust. Unless there is respect for the other person or group, there will be no respect for their knowledge.

Once again this is tightly linked to the broader cultural values of the organisation. This should be a value that is important to the broader organisation to enable knowledge management to work well. If not, it is normally found that knowledge is created and shared in certain isolated areas of the organisation where respect and trust have formed

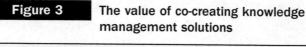

Figure 3   The value of co-creating knowledge management solutions

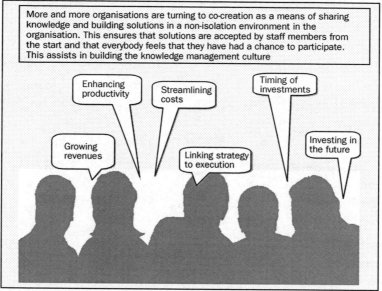

through a natural process. This does, however, lead to fragmentation of knowledge and a lack of integration, which has a negative impact on the flow of knowledge. This is especially the case where there is rivalry between departments in an organisation, or where animosity between areas in the organisation exists.

Respect is also an issue between different age groups and between different hierarchical levels in the organisation. Often, staff higher up in the hierarchy do not respect junior staff enough to share knowledge with them. The same goes for differences in age – it is often found that older generation staff do not share knowledge with junior staff members, as they feel that their knowledge will not be respected.

Respect and trust really go hand in hand and are two values that need to be addressed together to enable a knowledge management programme to make great strides forward.

Recognition

Recognition is an important value in any knowledge management programme. Individuals want to be recognised for their contributions to knowledge management programmes, whether that is the creation of knowledge in the form of innovations, the sharing of knowledge, the harvesting of knowledge or the leveraging of knowledge in order to improve the efficiency of the organisation.

Recognition and reward often go hand in hand, but are distinctly different. Recognition means that people want to be valued for their role and their contributions in the knowledge management value chain. Recognition may mean verbal recognition such as recognition at an awards event, in a newsletter, on an intranet, via e-mail, etc. Recognition may also be more tangible through monetary reward such as increasing a staff member's salary, awarding a bonus or a one-off prize.

The key, however, is, that most people do not mind sharing what they know, as long as their knowledge, skills and abilities are recognised by those on the receiving end, or those in the environment where the knowledge is shared. People want to feel like valued members of a team that deliver valuable intellectual capital contributions.

Reward

Rewards and incentives are crucial to the success of knowledge management (Darling, 2000; Greco, 1999; Hargaddon & Sutton, 2000; Reiss, 1999). It creates a climate of co-operation, learning and innovation. Incentives and rewards are crucial to knowledge management. Knowledge management programme managers are of the opinion that incentives and rewards create and support positive behaviours. They also point out that in organisations these incentives and rewards have been successfully tied to salaries and bonuses. Knowledge creation, sharing, harvesting and leveraging can be encouraged by tying them to job evaluations and performance measurement. In general, recognition for participation is essential. Some organisations are weary of monetary rewards, and would rather embed knowledge management activities as a cultural norm that has its own intrinsic value. Whatever the nature and structure of the programme, it is imperative that it is visible within the organisation.

Incentives and rewards are crucial to the success of a knowledge management programme. In a knowledge-based society, people see knowledge on a particular subject as a competitive advantage, and it would therefore be contrary to their nature to share this knowledge without some sort of incentive. In most organisations, a culture of knowledge hoarding, or 'knowledge is power', prevails. The reward and incentive system for knowledge management should consist of push and pull rewards, e.g. rewarding people as part of their performance appraisals according to participation in the programme (push) and incentivising people to use the knowledge base to provide a platform for their innovative ideas, i.e. providing them and their ideas with visibility in the organisation (pull).

Reciprocation

The value of reciprocation is invaluable in making a knowledge management programme effective. It is a natural human process that people will share knowledge with those willing to share knowledge back with them. Where knowledge sharing is a one way process, people feel they are not recognised for their contributions and neither are they rewarded by getting something back in return. Therefore, they usually stop participating in the knowledge management programme.

Reciprocation is one of the most important values to instil in the knowledge management programme. The culture of the organisation will definitely influence the culture of the knowledge management programme in this instance. If the organisational environment and culture is a very transparent, open, caring and sharing type of environment, two-way knowledge sharing is usually not a problem. However, if these values are not instilled in the organisational culture, it tends to become a problem with respect to knowledge management. One-way knowledge sharing is a quick way of stopping knowledge flow.

This also ties into the 'knowledge is power' syndrome where people tend to keep knowledge for themselves as a powerbase and do not share it, or only share it selectively to certain people. The issue of reciprocation can often not be fixed on the level of knowledge management culture, but on the level of organisational culture. As stated earlier, a transparent environment is crucial to ensure that knowledge flows quickly and easily throughout the organisation. If there is no transparency, but a culture of knowledge hoarding without reciprocation, knowledge sharing will not take place.

Knowledge sharing valued as organisation contribution

Knowledge sharing by individuals is often not viewed by managers as a true contribution to the organisation. It is viewed as something that is just done as part of the way they work. Though it is true that knowledge flows within processes and is therefore technically part of the way people work, knowledge creation, sharing, harvesting and leveraging activities must be acknowledged as separate activities by leadership teams in the organisation. It should be identified and rewarded as a unique contribution to the agility and competitive edge of the organisation.

It ties back to the need for reward and recognition. People want to feel that they make a contribution to the organisation when they create knowledge or share what they know. They need to feel that their contributions to the organisational body of knowledge are needed and respected, and form part of a valued set of intellectual capital that will be used by more than one person through, for example, communities of practice.

Knowledge sharing value proposition for the individual

As individuals, people work hard to gain specialist knowledge. There are two schools of thinking around sharing knowledge, especially specialist knowledge, on an individual basis, and this is basically tied to an individual's personal values.

The first school of thinking finds that people are happy to share their knowledge as it heightens their profile as an expert within their field and within their organisation. They therefore get acknowledgement and recognition for it. Knowledge creation, sharing, harvesting and leveraging is therefore never an obstacle in their environment. This scenario is usually found where reward and recognition structures are in place.

The second school of thinking finds that people are not willing to share their knowledge due to the 'knowledge is power' phenomenon where they feel that their knowledge gives them a competitive edge above what others in the organisation know, and they therefore do not want to share that knowledge. This scenario is usually found where reward and recognition structures are not in place.

Essentially, individuals earn their knowledge the hard way and when they do share it, they feel that there has to be 'something in it for them'. This is basic human psychology and a knowledge management programme should be designed so that it can cater to satisfy the individual value proposition. This is not always easy, as many different values drive different people, but the individual value proposition must be recognised and satisfied (see Figure 4).

Common goals and a common organisational structure

The organisational culture impacts the implementation of knowledge management largely by having common goals and having a common organisational structure (O'Dell & Grayson, 1999). Goals and objectives usually influence the execution of the business process value chain of the

Figure 4   The individual value proposition for sharing knowledge

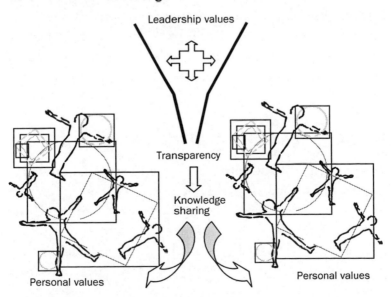

Leadership values

Transparency

Knowledge sharing

Personal values

Personal values

organisation. An organisation's knowledge management programme is largely built around its business process value chain and therefore the goals and objectives of the organisation are of the essence in the knowledge management programme. It is important that these objectives work together to achieve a common goal, which in turn will achieve the business strategy of the organisation. The culture created by this structure will focus the knowledge management programme.

The organisational structure is extremely important with respect to flow of knowledge in the organisation. The organisational structure is often responsible for creating silos in the organisation and encouraging silo behaviour, which means that free flow of knowledge is impeded and the culture of knowledge sharing is hampered. It is therefore very important that the organisational structure is carefully evaluated to ensure that optimal knowledge creation and sharing can take place. A flat organisational structure has been found to be very effective to ensure knowledge flow both horizontally between colleagues, but also vertically between hierarchical managerial staff levels. Where there isn't a flat structure, this should be taken into account in the design of the programme and it should be foreseen that the organisational structure may bring silo behaviour to the fore.

Acknowledgement of personal work pride

When sharing knowledge, it is extremely important to recognise the individual's personal work pride. The recognition of people's work pride goes hand in hand with their willingness and openness to create and share knowledge in the organisation. This also goes hand in hand with the individual value proposition for knowledge creation and sharing. If the individual gets no acknowledgement for the knowledge that he or she creates and/or shares, that person might start falling into the other, 'knowledge is power' category of staff members that feel that they are not willing to share their knowledge, because they see it as an individual resource and not a collective, organisational resource.

It is important for the knowledge management programme to recognise this and design the programme according to these behaviours, as this can make or break the success of the knowledge management programme. It is much better to know the behaviour of the individuals in an organisation upfront in order to plan ahead, than to find it out later once the knowledge management programme has been implemented.

Measurement issues

Linking the value of knowledge management to individual performance, as a driver of knowledge management culture

If knowledge management in the organisation is not linked to the individual's performance with respect to knowledge management activities such as the creation, sharing, harvesting and leveraging of knowledge, it could impact negatively on the implementation of a knowledge management programme in the organisation (PricewaterhouseCoopers, 1999). Knowledge is often seen by individuals as something that they own and that provides them with a competitive edge, and therefore do not want to share it. They therefore become part of the 'knowledge is power' syndrome and then withhold knowledge from the rest of the organisation.

It is therefore crucial to ensure that individuals are measured in their performance contracts on knowledge management activities that they participate in. This incentivises people to participate in the knowledge management programme, and it is a yardstick for the organisation to indicate in which areas certain problems or issues may be arising, e.g. silo behaviour may be found only in certain areas of the organisation. This will assist in designing solutions to rectify any problems or issues that crop up.

It is not always easy to measure an individuals' contribution to a knowledge management programme. Some examples that organisations have used are the number of contributions to centres of excellence repositories. An argument that many people have against this measure is, for example, that the number is not necessarily indicative of the quality of the contribution. Once one starts moving into qualitatively evaluating contributions to a knowledge base, specialists are required for evaluation, which is often a problem with respect to time. There are many examples of measuring individuals' performance in knowledge management programmes, and each of these would be different in different organisations, as the goals and objectives of the knowledge management programme in each organisation will differ. The behaviour and culture of the individuals in the organisation will also differ and therefore the measurements will be suited to adapt to these in each specific organisation.

Once again it can be seen that there is no real way to have a knowledge management implementation blueprint, due to the diversity of cultural aspects in the organisation having such a huge impact on the knowledge management programme.

Incorporating knowledge management into specific key performance indicators of the organisation is overseen, e.g. the Balanced Score Card

The knowledge management programme, as well as the resulting efficiencies attained in processes and practices, needs to be measured. The performance of the overall knowledge management initiative needs to be measured, as well as the management of the knowledge itself. The performance measurement may include reviews of the knowledge repositories and giving visible rewards to those who show commitment to the knowledge management programme.

The impact knowledge management has must be measured to enable tracking of successes and failures. Knowledge management is not a static activity and grows with the organisation as it changes, and therefore impact should be continuously assessed to ensure that knowledge management is keeping up with current needs in the organisation. Some organisations measure their knowledge management systems' success on the number of entries made into repositories, as well as the number of times a knowledge repository or a specific document was accessed. They also do periodic qualitative reviews of the knowledge management programme through use of surveys and questionnaires. Other organisations tie their knowledge management measures into their organisational balanced scorecard. In that way, knowledge and knowledge management is seen to make a definitive impact on the strategic management of the organisation and it can be actively managed on a quarterly basis. It allows the business to draw up specific action plans on how they can more effectively utilise and manage knowledge as an organisational resource.

Linking the value of knowledge management to the performance of groups and teams creates a knowledge management culture

Linking the value of knowledge management to the performance of groups and teams creates a knowledge management culture in the organisation. Cultural realities in an organisation need to be taken into account when implementing knowledge management. Once these cultural realities have been identified, a vision needs to be formulated encompassing the need to succeed despite these realities as well as the fact that managing knowledge will help the organisation to achieve its goals. It is imperative to link knowledge management to culture and personal as well as organisational values via the values emanating from groups and teams such as communities of practice, communities of interest, and centres of excellence.

As individuals are measured on their knowledge management performance, teams and groups should also be measured to identify their collective contributions to the organisation's knowledge base. The old adage still remains true – what gets measured, gets done. In specific areas of specialisation, it is incentivising for teams to be measured on their collective knowledge management behaviour and the unique culture they create amongst themselves. It also ensures that there are linkages and communication amongst these groups that break down silo behaviour.

Knowledge management programmes depend on cultural and behavioural change, which occur more slowly than business process change. Organisations with a viable strategy, adequate funding and specific knowledge management skills can implement knowledge management support with minimal difficulty. However, this only lays a foundation on which culture and behaviours can evolve. The real effort and risk in knowledge management is building participation in knowledge management. The initial work to implement knowledge management support may be short, but participation, culture and behaviour may take many years to reach an optimum state.

Moving to a culture that values and encourages innovation, openness, teamwork and knowledge sharing, requires leadership, as well as changes in relationships and organisational structures in the office environment. Management must consider what needs to be done to effect this change. Sustainable cultural change takes time, but useful initiatives can be kicked off quite quickly, e.g. creating communities of practice.

Organisations are too operationally focused to allow time for knowledge management

In most organisations, managers, especially middle management, are so operationally focused in getting the daily job done, that tasks like knowledge management tasks fall by the wayside. For those working in the organisation, there is always something that takes priority above knowledge management. It is seen as an administrative task, not as something that is embedded into their day to day tasks. This creates an issue, as in these cases the knowledge management activities frequently just don't get done. It is often due to a lack of understanding of management of the critical role that knowledge and knowledge management plays in the organisation and how strategically valuable it is in order to increase the agility and the efficiency of the organisation.

This is especially true in professional services or other services organisations where, for example, people are measured against time spent per client. They are only rewarded for that time and not rewarded for time spent on activities that build the organisation's value, such as knowledge management. Once again, reward structures come to the fore as being very important in creating the correct knowledge creation, sharing, harvesting and leveraging behaviour in the organisation. Time has to be allocated per week to allow people to participate in knowledge management activities, and they should not be penalised for spending that time on knowledge management activities. That time should be seen as being as valuable as the time spent on client focused activities. It is a mindset change that needs to take place in the organistion and in the mind of the leadership team and the staff.

Strategy and leadership

Buy-in from top down structures can ensure organisational buy-in

Top management support is essential for successful knowledge management. Leaders have to share a vision on knowledge management and provide such a programme with ongoing support. Leaders have to be continually briefed on the knowledge management programme and what it entails, and how it is going to achieve the agreed knowledge management vision. Leaders have to lead by example.

The role of top management is crucial. Top management support of knowledge management will enforce the message that knowledge management is linked to the execution of the organisational strategy. It is, however, important to ensure that top management understands what knowledge management is about and what benefits it will bring to the organisation. Top management should initiate a knowledge management programme, fully realising what they are asking for and what it will entail. This will ensure that they will be getting a solution they expect. This is due to the fact that they could verbalise their requirements at the outset of the programme. Communication about the deliverables of such a programme to top management from the start is very important to ensure that what is being delivered by the knowledge management programme is clear to everyone involved (Temkin, 2001).

It is not only important for top management to understand what the knowledge management programme entails, but also how the organisational culture, and specifically the organisational strategy, will impact it. A knowledge management strategy is always tied to an organisational strategy and cannot be separated, and therefore it is important for top managers to understand how integrated knowledge management really fits in with other activities in the business process value chain of the organisation. It is not a separate function, but in fact an integral part of the work that is performed in the organisation. This message should be communicated top down by management to the employees in the organisation.

In addition to top management support, knowledge management champions or sponsors have to be identified throughout the organisation to be evangelists and role models within the programme. The higher the level of sponsorship, the greater the chances of success for the programme.

New economy leadership is essential to create a culture conducive for knowledge management

Knowledge management is a new economy concept. Although it has been around for a number of years, it is still considered to be a new economy concept which requires a new economy mindset and new economy thinking.

To enable that, new economy leadership is required to ensure that a culture conducive for knowledge management is created. It is sometimes very difficult to change old economy thinking to new economy thinking and to implement new ideas into old environments, where people have very fixed ideas of how things have worked in the past and how things should work because that is the way they have always worked.

An organisation therefore needs an innovative leadership team to implement and promote the concept of knowledge management to ensure that the concept obtains the level of buy-in required from staff to ensure a successful implementation. Staff must be made aware of this new economy concept and how it adds new value in a new economy in today's working world, and what impact it has on their daily working life. They should also be made aware of the potential impact on the organisation with respect to increased agility and improved decision making ability.

A lot of organisations have failed attempts at knowledge management implementations due to the fact that they have old economy leaders who have trouble trying to propagate new economy concepts in their respective organisations. The intended messages about the value proposition thereof therefore never really reach the staff, which means that they never really understand the individual value proposition of knowledge management. The effect thereof is that knowledge management implementations fail partially or completely due to the value proposition message being lost.

A decentralised knowledge management leadership function will lead to disjointed knowledge management endeavours

A lot of organisations have specific approaches to centralisation or decentralisation of specific functions. This has very important consequences for knowledge management, as it will have an impact on the efficiency of the implementation of knowledge management in the organisation.

In most organisations, a decentralised approach towards knowledge management leads to a silo approach in the creation, sharing, harvesting, and leveraging of knowledge management. This is especially true if it is done per department or specialist area in the organisation. Complete centralisation also does not work entirely as a centralised function does not always understand the unique needs of each of the departments or specialist areas, making it very difficult to manage their knowledge effectively.

Organisations globally have found that a hybrid approach usually works the best. Organisations usually have knowledge needs that are shared across the organisation, e.g. knowledge on strategy, processes, organisational structures, human resources and technology. This knowledge can be managed and made available centrally to all people in the organisation. Then there are departments, areas of specialisation, or communities of practice, communities of interest, centres of excellence, etc, that have very specific knowledge that they work with that may not be of interest or use to the wider audience in the organisation. This knowledge may then be managed and made available in a decentralised way only to those who would have an interest in it or who could use it in their daily work environment.

Each organisation has its own unique needs with respect to what their needs are in terms of centralisation vs. decentralisation vs. a hybrid model. It is sometimes only through practical implementation and trial and error that the optimal solution for the organisation can be identified. Once again it is clear that there is no real blueprint for the implementation of knowledge management, because it is dependent on the culture of the organisation itself (see Figure 5).

Absence of defined roles, leadership and ownership can lead to no leadership at all

The absence of defined roles, leadership and ownership of business programmes in an organisation can lead to an absence of leadership. The definition of these leadership roles is extremely important and must be viewed as a critical success factor for knowledge management. Knowledge management

Figure 5 Centralisation vs. decentralisation of the knowledge management programme

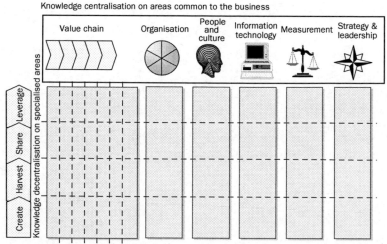

pervades the whole organisation, and knowledge management leaders have to work closely with business leaders in specific areas in the business. The identification of roles, leadership and ownership is therefore essential for the knowledge management programme in an organisation to ensure that there are points of contact or 'gatekeepers' in the business who can assist in instilling the knowledge management programme as well as culture in the organisation. These are business people who are not part of the knowledge management programme, but act as gatekeepers or links.

The need for defined roles, leadership and ownership is also true within the knowledge management programme. There should be clear ownership and leadership of the programme, with staff members with clearly defined roles and responsibilities. These people will be responsible for the implementation of knowledge in the organisation and embedding the knowledge management culture into the organisation.

Operational issues

An organisational strategy is essential to inform a knowledge management strategy which in turn is essential to direct a knowledge management culture

It is critical that the knowledge management strategy is tied to the organisational strategy. Knowledge management should never be implemented as an end in itself. Knowledge management programmes succeed when knowledge capital is employed to accomplish specific organisational strategies. Very few knowledge management programmes are not tied to a specific business strategy or goal. Managing knowledge is no different from managing other aspects of an organisation: firstly, there must be a vision that links with the organisation's objectives and strategies; secondly, people must be aligned with that vision; and thirdly, the alignment must be from the top down and across the organisation.

It is critical for a knowledge management programme to be based on an organisation's processes and activities to ensure that knowledge is optimised to build the critical capabilities of the organisation. Tying the knowledge management programme to an organisation's business processes will ensure that the programme is oriented towards achieving efficiency improvements within core and enabling processes through more effective and efficient use of knowledge, thus assisting in achieving the objectives of the organisational strategy. Business processes are always tied to the organisional strategy, making them a logical starting point for a knowledge management strategy and programme, and thus ensuring that the knowledge management strategy supports the organisational strategy and does not exist in isolation.

A knowledge management strategy is crucial to the success of a knowledge management programme. The knowledge management strategy should address a variety of issues. Firstly, the creation of understanding of the organisation's knowledge resources should be addressed. This will allow the organisation to set up a knowledge management agenda through which knowledge can be leveraged optimally. Assessing knowledge resources leads to shaping of the knowledge agenda to achieve sustainable results in alignment with the organisational strategy. The agenda determines how the organisation must leverage the knowledge to achieve breakthrough results. It is essential to have an integrated view of the organisation's strategy, people, leadership, process, technology and metrics if positive results are to be attained. A knowledge management agenda is critical to achieve desired outcomes, mobilising the organisation and establishing critical performance measures. It is essential to create an implementation and daily maintenance plan of knowledge management within the organisation. This is essential in understanding how knowledge can enhance and enable specific processes in the organisation.

Secondly, the knowledge management strategy needs to articulate the role that knowledge will play in creating value for the organisation. The vision also needs to consider resource availability with respect to people and financing, as this focuses the implementation approach.

Thirdly, the strategy should be comprised of a number of integrated projects, phased in over time. These initiatives should include quick wins as well as long-term plans and activities. The knowledge management strategy should clearly link to business objectives and encompass a vision of short-term and long-term initiatives and benefits. A knowledge management strategy is usually executed as a process, not a project. Knowledge management is not a static activity, but an ongoing activity.

Finally, the knowledge management strategy should also indicate the risks associated with a knowledge management programme in the organisation.

To conclude, the knowledge management strategy should contain the vision, mission and objectives of the knowledge management programme. It should also contain a value proposition, critical success factors and risks. All of these must be presented within the organisational context and its specific issues, to ensure that the knowledge management strategy is tied to the organisational strategy (see Figure 6).

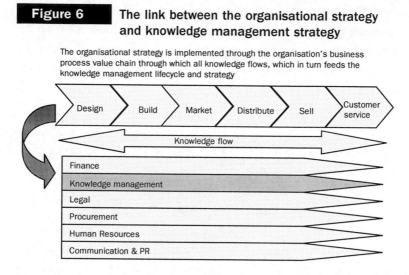

Figure 6 — The link between the organisational strategy and knowledge management strategy

The organisational strategy is implemented through the organisation's business process value chain through which all knowledge flows, which in turn feeds the knowledge management lifecycle and strategy

Duplication of knowledge takes place through silo ownership

Knowledge management leads to less reinvention of the wheel, i.e. duplication of work which is often caused by working in silos, through the use of knowledge in different contexts. For example, the same presentation or proposal may have been recreated by different teams of people in an organisation many times due to the lack of sharing of knowledge. Identifying what works best requires effort and discipline, but the knowledge management programme can then replicate these practices throughout the organisation. The better this is executed, the more competitive the organisation will be.

Reusing knowledge in different contexts stimulates staff to improve on past solutions, or to create new knowledge, thereby creating a culture of innovation. This enhances the knowledge management value chain and enhances the flow of knowledge through the organisation. Through innovation a culture of knowledge creation is stimulated, which kicks off the knowledge management process value chain. This is a stimulus for communities of practice, for example.

Once again, the organisational culture of a silo mentality can directly impact the knowledge management programme by creating an environment where knowledge is duplicated. The knowledge management programme leaders therefore have to take cognisance of this fact and try to counterbalance duplication by strengthening the knowledge management value chain as far as possible.

Knowledge management illiteracy exists because people are often not trained on knowledge management and what it entails

Organisations often implement knowledge where all of the staff are almost totally illiterate with respect to knowledge management. Organisational culture is not often oriented towards communication, learning and training and therefore the knowledge management programme is not embedded in the organisational culture.

It is crucial for organisations that have knowledge management programmes to ensure that their staff are properly trained on what the concept of knowledge management entails, and what the value proposition of it is for both the individual as well as for the organisation. A staff member needs training on the philosophy of knowledge management, on knowledge management processes and what value they add, how knowledge management technology works and enables the programme, what communities of practice and interest are, etc. They need to be taken through a formal training course and preferably this training course should be compulsory and presented to staff members when they join the organisation. This will ensure that they benefit from the knowledge management programme from the day that they start working at the organisation. Knowledge management training should preferably be part of a person's induction training upon joining the organisation. Refresher courses should also be available for staff that have been at the organisation for longer periods of time and who would like to update their knowledge and skills.

Communities are not identified, defined and formalised, therefore knowledge is not shared in a formalised way

Knowledge creation, sharing, harvesting and leveraging mostly takes place very informally in organisations. This is due to the fact that most organisations do not have formal knowledge management programmes, and therefore knowledge communities are not identified, defined and formalised as part of the culture of the organisation (Hickins, 1999). Communities of practice and communities of interest may exist, but in a very informal way, and run according to very informal rules.

This does not mean that valuable knowledge is not created and shared in these communities. However, the knowledge is often in tacit format and no record is kept of its existence. In a more formalised knowledge management environment a culture of communities of practice and communities of interest can be created, where knowledge can be created and shared in a more structured way on specific platforms created for that purpose. It can thus be shared in a more explicit format than before and it can be shared to a wider audience than before. This increases the added value that the organisation can get from the knowledge shared in these communities.

Work is often duplicated due to the 'not created here' culture

Knowledge can be duplicated because people often do not want to take up knowledge in their working community due to the fact that they did not create it themselves and that it was not part of their own innovative thinking processes (Gordon & Smith, 2006). People feel that they want to create their own solutions and that they want to be recognised and rewarded for these contributions. This need can be based on an individual, team or group basis. It is seen as 'not invented here' knowledge and is therefore discarded, even though it may be valuable.

This is often an issue when an organisation has a silo based culture, where different areas in the organisation either operate very differently or have a very unique culture. Knowledge flow between these silos is not necessarily strained, but the use of the knowledge, once received, can be hampered. This can have a negative impact on the organisation as this may lead to duplication of work, or the knowledge can be totally discarded, which leads to inefficiencies in the organisation's processes which in turn lead to increases in costs. It may not only lead to duplication of work, but also lead to disparate thinking with respect to strategy between different areas of the organisation, which may be damaging to the organisation in itself.

Some equate this to the 'knowledge is power' syndrome, but it is actually something quite different. It is a movement more around the ownership of the creation of knowledge and recognition of ownership of knowledge, whilst 'knowledge is power' is more about the hesitance to share knowledge.

Organisations often allocate too few resources for knowledge management

Knowledge management is a new economy concept and often not well understood by the organisations implementing it. Due to the lack of understanding of the concept and what implementation of it entails, organisations often allocate too few resources for knowledge management endeavours. These resources include monetary resources, people and technology.

The resources required by each organisation will be unique. It will be unique with respect to what is already in place vs. what needs to be put into place, whether knowledge management is budgeted for in the organisational (strategic and operational) budget, whether needs have correctly been identified and whether a cost/benefit study has been done.

Only once an appropriate business case has been built by the knowledge management team can the correct amount of resources be allocated by the organisation's management team to the knowledge management programme. This business case has to contain at least the following information: vision, mission, objectives, drivers, critical success factors, implementation roadmap, resources required (people, technology, process, strategy), risks and mitigating actions, assumptions, stakeholders, role players, funding required, measures of success and governance.

The business case will assist the management of the organisation to understand what the funding will be used for and will allow them to be more willing to allocate the funds to the programme if they know exactly what the resources will be spent on. This should be done at least on an annual basis. It also allows the knowledge management team to reflect back on their business case at the end of the year to see if they have achieved the goals they set out to.

A limited understanding exists of the end to end value chain of knowledge management

In most organisations that have implemented knowledge management, a limited understanding exists of the end to end value chain of knowledge management. Organisations do not seem to grasp that, as they have a business process value chain, they also have a knowledge management process value chain.

To fully implement a knowledge management programme successfully, an in-depth understanding of the knowledge management value chain of the organisation is required. This spans all activities, from when knowledge is created through to when it is leveraged. It is important to understand these activities to enable the maximisation of the value of the activities. It is also important in order to assign roles for management of these activities in the organisation. The knowledge management value chain is also crucial in ensuring that there is no silo effect in the organisation where knowledge flow is hampered, and it should show up weak points in the value chain where knowledge flow is impeded. This allows the knowledge management team to keep a close eye on the flow of knowledge in the organisation to ensure that no knowledge flow blockages take place.

Limited integration of knowledge can lead to a lack of knowledge sharing across internal organisational boundaries

Knowledge and knowledge management is used to build common denominators across functional groups in organisations, thereby streamlining internal integration. Knowledge management facilitates transparency and therefore assists in organisational integration. If there is a limited amount of integration of knowledge in the organisation, especially across boundaries, it can lead to a lack of knowledge sharing.

Knowledge management facilitates knowledge integration through creation of knowledge sharing platforms such as intranets, communities of practice, and centres of excellence.

It also facilitates knowledge sharing through its knowledge management business process value chain. If these components of the knowledge management programme are not in place, knowledge sharing will not take place effectively.

Organisations with silo-based knowledge sharing behaviour therefore already show behaviour of a lack of integration, a lack of usage of the knowledge management business process value chain and a lack of effective usage of knowledge management platforms. The organisational culture therefore gives clues as to the status of the knowledge management programme in the organisation.

Security of knowledge is crucial in the knowledge management environment

Organisational culture dictates how important the organisation views information and knowledge security to be. The first point to make here is that some organisations are more knowledge based than others. A management consultancy would be more knowledge based than a tyre repair shop, for example. These knowledge based businesses will, from a cultural point of view, place a lot of emphasis on the security of their knowledge and information. This is true for both electronic knowledge and information as well as paper based knowledge and information.

Organisations that are security conscious will ensure that their computer networks have security features built into their knowledge sharing systems and cannot be accessed by unauthorised persons. They will ensure that regular back-ups are made. They will also ensure that important documentation is not lying unguarded around the office where it is easily accessible. Industrial espionage is rife in the business world, and organisations must be very aware that they should protect their knowledge and intellectual capital from the outside world. It could negatively impact their competitive edge in the marketplace if strategic knowledge and information are leaked.

Lack of cross-skilling takes place due to the silo effect

Organisational structures may prevent knowledge from flowing freely in the organisation, and due to this knowledge silos are created in the organisation. This, however, has a larger impact than just the knowledge silos that are being created and the prevention of knowledge flow across departmental boundaries. The lack of knowledge flow also has an impact on cross-skilling in the organisation. If knowledge does not flow to different areas of the business, cross-skilling is usually limited. This impacts the learning and development of the organisation's staff members negatively simply because they do not have access to knowledge on an informal basis to cross-skill and up-skill themselves.

One of the outcomes of the silo effect and the lack of cross-skilling can also be a competitive effect between different areas in the business, that start to compete based on performance. Access to knowledge and cross-skilling will be a competitive factor and will definitely in turn affect the organisation's culture.

The negative impact of duplication of knowledge

Organisations often have no knowledge management programmes in place. The knowledge management lifecycle is not managed, which leads to knowledge being duplicated in the organisation. This is very inefficient and costly for the organisation, as time and effort is being duplicated by staff members in various areas of the organisation.

Knowledge management leads to less reinvention of the wheel, i.e. duplication of work, through the re-use of knowledge in different contexts. Reusing knowledge stimulates staff to improve on past solutions or to create new knowledge, thereby creating a culture of innovation.

The importance of access to paper based information

A number of organisations may have knowledge management programmes providing access to electronically captured knowledge and information, but not paper-based information and knowledge. The organisational culture is such that it has no focus on or puts no value on paper-based knowledge and information. This precludes people in the organisation from a wealth of knowledge.

The organisational culture may need to change and be made aware of the fact that paper-based knowledge and information has value and should not be left out of the equation when looking at a knowledge management programme, even though access and storage may be difficult.

Processes

Embedding knowledge management processes is essential in creating a knowledge management culture

Knowledge management is often implemented as a separate administrative function in an organisation and not as an integral part of the business. This is not an effective decision as knowledge flows within processes and processes are part of the core business process value chain that is essentially there to execute the organisational strategy. Knowledge management should, therefore, be implemented as an embedded part of the knowledge management and organisational culture of the organisation by making it an integral part of the way people work on a daily basis and not by making it something 'extra' that they have to do over and above their normal workload (Kennedy, 1996; Gordon & Smith, 2006).

This is also why it is suggested that knowledge management measurements be built into staff performance measurements as with any other tasks they do, so that it is not seen as something different or out of the ordinary, but part of their daily routine.

If knowledge is not embedded into the daily work routine, it is very difficult to get people to participate. The reward and recognition issues become more difficult to handle and it becomes more difficult to drive knowledge management as a strategic programme in the organisation. It will have a much more operational flavour and will carry less importance in the minds of staff members. The organisational culture will thus immediately influence the success of the knowledge management programme.

Perceived fragmentation/diversity and needs makes process mapping in the knowledge management environment complex

There is often a perceived fragmentation or diversity of needs with respect to knowledge management in the organisation. This is true in a number of ways, but should not be seen as a negative in the knowledge management programme. The needs are often very similar, but are just viewed from a different angle.

The first differentiation lies in how people create, share, harvest and leverage knowledge on an individual and team level. The knowledge management programme should be able to cater for all three these levels, as they all share knowledge in a different way and their needs with respect to knowledge management differ. Individuals share knowledge differently than teams do.

The next differentiation is between different hierarchical levels in the organisation. People on different hierarchical levels tend to share knowledge very differently. It is often found that middle management, for example, are often the staff members with the 'knowledge is power' mindset, whilst the top and lower levels share knowledge freely. Top management will share by necessity, often due to time constraints. Usually, the less hierarchy in the organisation, the better the knowledge flow.

Finally, there is a differentiation in the way different areas or divisions in an organisation create, share, harvest and leverage knowledge. This is due to the particular culture of that area or division. Some areas share very freely, whilst others do not. This may be due to a number of factors, such as leadership, the use of technology, training, etc.

Processes to codify tacit knowledge to explicit knowledge is important to ensure that 'invisible' part of the organisation is captured

Knowledge can be defined as interpreted information put into action through use in processes, procedures, documents and repositories, to add value to the resulting activity of an individual, team or organisation. Knowledge can be split into two distinct categories, namely tacit knowledge and explicit knowledge. Tacit knowledge is defined as a combination of skills, experiences, perceptions and expertise that is hard to articulate and codify, and it mostly resides in people's heads. Explicit knowledge can be defined as knowledge that can be shared through and captured in a common language.

It is important to differentiate between these types of knowledge, as knowledge management addresses each differently. Knowledge management's focus is more on tacit knowledge and the transformation of tacit into explicit knowledge, than it is on explicit knowledge. This is one of the most distinguishing factors between knowledge management and information management. If the role of, e.g. communities of practice, is researched, it is clear that the purpose thereof is the sharing of tacit knowledge in the form of experiences, skills and intuition. This is also true of discussion forums, newsgroups, etc. Although the sharing of explicit knowledge in these forums cannot be ruled out, the focus is more on tacit knowledge.

Knowledge management, however, also addresses explicit knowledge in the form of making documents, manuals, and forms containing knowledge, articles, etc. available through mechanisms such as intranets, extranets and databases. It also assists in the creation of these documents or knowledge nuggets, as well as in the indexing, storage, retrieval, application and destruction thereof.

Explicit knowledge is easier to manage than tacit knowledge. Once knowledge is made explicit, it is easier to get the creator of the knowledge to share it, either through giving it away to someone else, or via selling it to someone at a cost. Once explicit it is easy to make it available for retrieval through indexing and/or taxonomy creation and logging it onto a database, intranet or other electronic platform. It can also be shared in paper-based format.

On the other hand, if an organisation has a number of employees with very valuable knowledge, and this knowledge is not made explicit, it can be very difficult for the organisation to manage that knowledge in terms of identification, categorisation or indexing, and sharing. These individuals may choose to leave the organisation with the knowledge, whereby it is lost to the organisation that has not managed to turn it into explicit knowledge, available in a codified format to others. To get individuals to translate their tacit knowledge into explicit knowledge is, however, often a difficult process. People still cling to the view that 'knowledge is power' and are therefore often reluctant to part with it.

Often these individuals need to be incentivised in some way to translate their tacit knowledge into explicit knowledge. Incentivising people to share knowledge, in tacit or explicit format, is critical to the success of the knowledge management programme. Examples of such incentives and rewards are tying knowledge sharing and participation in the knowledge management programme to the annual performance appraisal of a staff member. Other ways are to give prizes, e.g. weekends away. Recognition through newsletters or announcements at staff meetings is also ways to incentivise people to share knowledge.

However, even incentives and rewards may still not be enough to encourage individuals to part with their knowledge. Once individuals decide to translate their tacit knowledge into explicit knowledge, it must be taken into account that a percentage of knowledge will be 'lost' in the explicit account, as tacit knowledge can never be translated one hundred percent accurately, as it is based on beliefs, intuition and perceptions.

The challenge of knowledge management therefore lies in creating and managing processes, platforms and mechanisms through which tacit knowledge can be managed per se, through which it can be translated to explicit knowledge as effectively as possible, and through which explicit knowledge can be managed using a structured approach (Du Plessis, 2003).

No visible process leadership will lead to processes not being implemented fully

Knowledge management processes, policies and procedures are crucial for any knowledge management programme. Processes can be subdivided into two areas of importance, namely knowledge management processes and associated knowledge management roles. It is critical to understand how knowledge is captured, evaluated, cleansed, stored, provided and used, and how the organisation can improve these processes in alignment with the knowledge management vision. Roles have to be created to perform the knowledge management processes.

Establishing processes relevant to all phases of the knowledge management lifecycle is very important, e.g. processes to create knowledge, processes to share knowledge and processes to harvest knowledge from either people or external sources. Knowledge management is a holistic solution comprising of processes, technology, culture and organisational structure. If any of these elements are not attended to, the knowledge management programme will fail. This is particularly true in the case of knowledge management processes. If an organisation, for example, has a very sophisticated technology based system, but there are no processes in place to manage the content in the system, the programme will fail as the content may become outdated, the quality may not be up to standard, etc. Processes provide structure and standards for the knowledge management programme and ensure that roles and responsibilities are clearly defined.

Knowledge management processes as well as business processes are an important part of any knowledge management programme. Processes, however, also need leaders to ensure that they are implemented properly, that they are integrated with other processes, that they are kept up to date, and that the governance around them is put into place. Leadership is also important to ensure that the knowledge management process value chain is integrated with the business process value chain of the organisation. This is important, as knowledge is part of the business that is done every day, and not a separate administrative function. Knowledge flows within processes and therefore processes play a key role in knowledge management. It is important, however, to have a process owner or process leader when knowledge management is implemented in an organisation to ensure that this key component is implemented effectively and integrated with the business process value chain.

Implementation of processes can be hampered by lack of common terminology

Organisational culture can influence a knowledge management programme if it is not likely to have a specific means of developing specific terms for specific concepts. Implementation of processes can be hampered by a lack of common terminology. Due to the fact that knowledge is a fairly new discipline, terminology has not necessarily been standardised. To ensure that knowledge implementations in the organisation go smoothly, common terminology needs to be developed. Staff need to be trained on knowledge management and therefore knowledge management terminology should be clearly defined and standardised. It is especially important with respect to processes due to the fact that processes are such a core and important part of any knowledge management programme.

Limited formal knowledge management processes often exist

A number of organisations often implement knowledge management without having formal knowledge management processes. This is often the downfall of these programmes. Knowledge management programmes need formally mapped processes that form part of a knowledge management value chain, which in turn fits into the organisation's business process value chain. Without formal knowledge management processes, managing the programme will be extremely difficult and formalisation thereof will be virtually impossible. Processes are probably the most important part of a knowledge management programme and therefore it is important to take time out to map them as part of the business process value chain, thus embedding it in the culture of the organisation.

Process buy-in from top down ensures the enforcing of the usage of knowledge management processes

Knowledge management processes not only require buy-in from the leaders of the knowledge management teams, but also from the top leaders of the organisation. There should be alignment with the organisational business process value chain to ensure efficiency in the flow of knowledge (Davenport, 1999). Leadership buy-in is crucial to ensure that implementation takes place, that activities take place and are followed by staff members, and that measurement on the execution of the processes can take place to ascertain the success of the knowledge management programme from a process point of view. If no buy-in is shown in the implementation of the processes, staff may show lack of interest in following them, and if their implementation is not measured, the programme success may be negatively impacted. Therefore, senior buy-in is essential.

Limited standard value chains for knowledge management processes exist

No two organisations' knowledge management process value chain will look exactly alike. Different organisations place different emphasis on different steps or phases in the value chain, from creation of knowledge through to the leveraging of knowledge. It is not incorrect to have different knowledge management process value chains – it shows the uniqueness of the organisation and its interaction knowledge as a fundamental resource. What is important, however, is to know what the value chain looks like and what the steps in the value chain are, so that they can be managed and so that they can be integrated with the organisation's larger business process value chain (see Figure 7).

Limited enterprise-wide standards exist for knowledge management process mapping

Some organisations have no standardised way of mapping their business process value chain. This will directly impact

| Figure 7 | The knowledge management business process value chain |

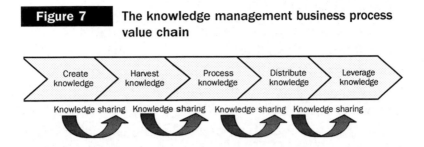

the knowledge management programme, as the knowledge management programme will also need to map its knowledge management processes. Once again the organisational culture can influence the knowledge management programme hugely.

If there is a standard set by the organisation, it is suggested that the knowledge management programme follow the same set of standards when mapping knowledge management processes to make integration easier. If there are no standards, the knowledge management programme should try and set a standard that can be used by the programme over a period of time and may even later be adopted by the organisation as whole as an organisational standard.

Standards are, however, very important when it comes to mapping of processes and this should be dictated either by the organisation or by the knowledge management programme.

Technology and other channels

Technology as enabler of knowledge management can enable or inhibit knowledge management culture

Dramatic changes in the way of working and developments in telecommunications and technology have made knowledge management increasingly important (Davenport, 1999).

Most organisations have high-speed networks and telecommunications infrastructure, which enable quick and efficient knowledge sharing. This leads to a requirement for organisations to manage the wealth of knowledge that is travelling through these high-speed networks and telecommunications technologies.

The fact that organisations implement technology thus acts as a catalyst for the implementation of knowledge management. Once again, the cultural decision of the organisation to go the technology route impacts the organisation on a knowledge management level.

Technology is a critical enabler for knowledge management. It ensures quick and efficient accessibility and availability of knowledge, as well as the searchability and manipulation thereof. It assists in facilitating the knowledge management lifecycle. It is crucial for any knowledge management programme to include infrastructure management – this does not only include technology, but also training and support. It is important that technical problems are sorted out prior to implementation and that adequate support measures are in place.

Staff members generate a wealth of information and knowledge as they move around technology systems both internally and externally to the organisation, such as on the intranet and the internet. Organisations are driven to implement knowledge management in order to harvest, organise, analyse and leverage this knowledge.

Lack of a single point of access to knowledge can lead to silo knowledge management behaviour and a lack of knowledge integration

Knowledge management provides easy access to knowledge, through a single point of entry, which enhances staff productivity. Individuals are able to find required and relevant knowledge, processes and people more quickly and efficiently. Knowledge management brings order to the knowledge base, thus enabling employees to find and focus on business- and task-relevant knowledge. This results in quicker and more effective decision making. Ease of access to knowledge will compress waiting time and work delays spent trying to find sources of knowledge. It therefore improves the agility of the organisation.

Technology plays a big part in providing a single point of access, e.g. through an intranet. If technology systems in an organisation are not integrated however, and there is no intranet present, technology can be an inhibitor in the retrieval of knowledge as staff members have to go and find knowledge in various technology based systems. This is time consuming and very inefficient from the users' point of view.

Taxonomies also provide a role in providing a single point of access. Through taxonomies, individuals can find a single point of access to the organisation's knowledge base through the representation of the knowledge base structure. Taxonomies are vital for a single point of access to the structure of the knowledge base. Technology based systems are structured, based on taxonomies (see Figure 8).

Understanding the value of technology with respect to technology management

Technology is one of the many tools in the knowledge management realm that adds value to the knowledge management programme. The truth is, however, that a lot of the time staff in organisations cannot see what particular value technology adds to creating a knowledge management culture.

Firstly, technology provides a platform where knowledge management can be created and shared amongst people in a variety of locations. It therefore allows sharing of

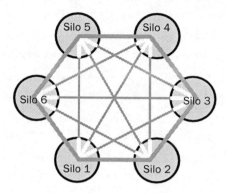

Figure 8 The lack of a single point of access to knowledge can lead to silo knowledge behavior or selective sharing between silos

knowledge between organisational boundaries, but also across organisational boundaries. It also allows knowledge bases to be searchable, making retrieval of knowledge much more effective and rapid. It provides a place for storage of knowledge and information in a structured way. It can assist in ensuring knowledge of a particular subject is pooled into one place, which makes it easier for the user to find: for example, in an online community of practice.

Technology also assists in extending the reach of knowledge. Through technology it is possible to share knowledge with people across the globe. Organisations can capitalise more efficiently on business opportunities anywhere in the world. Organisations can eliminate barriers that previously existed, expanding their customer and supplier base, and can operate in markets that have been out of bounds before through extension of the reach of their knowledge.

Lack of systems integration can lead to silo knowledge management behaviour

If systems in the organisation do not integrate, knowledge and information on these sytems also cannot integrate

(Kennedy, 1996). This leads to silo behaviour and a lack of knowledge integration between various areas of the business (Zyngier, 2006). A lack of integration means that knowledge is often duplicated in the organisation due to a lack of an overview of what is available in the organsiation.

In the eBusiness environment, collaboration is becoming increasingly prevalent. eBusinesses collaboratively design products across geographical boundaries and sometimes across organisational boundaries. There is also collaboration in the form of virtual communities internal and external to the organisation, e.g. through intranets and extranets. These communities share knowledge on a wide variety of issues. Knowledge management provides the technology, processes and platforms to enable the said collaboration. Knowledge management also ensures the retention and structuring of the knowledge shared in these collaborative forums that can be used as input to further knowledge creation within these and other forums.

Knowledge management also ensures that processes and platforms exist to convert tacit knowledge to explicit knowledge within knowledge exchanges in virtual communities or collaborative forums. Value can thus be extracted from tacit knowledge, and knowledge attrition can be minimised. As a result of collaborative design taking place across geographical and organisational boundaries through provision of collaboration forums and related knowledge management tools and processes, the organisation's time to market decreases and agility increases.

Knowledge management plays a role in facilitating communication through the provision of technology, processes and platforms that enable communication. Knowledge management also ensures the retention of knowledge shared in these communication forums for future use.

Lack of access to enabling technology

In organisations, staff do not always have access to the necessary technology to enable them to create, share, harvest and leverage knowledge. Although a knowledge management programme is not driven by technology, a knowledge management programme will never really get off the ground without people having access to appropriate technology. The management of the knowledge management programme should therefore ensure that all staff have access to the correct technology to enable them to do knowledge management at the level they need to be doing it.

That does not necessarily imply that all people will have exactly the same technology, as people may be working on different levels of skill, e.g. shop floor workers in a manufacturing environment vs. their colleagues in the management team of the organisation. It is therefore not always a straightforward rollout of a set of similar technologies across the organisation, but must be based on the individual needs of the user.

In some cases, organisations cannot afford e.g. PCs for every knowledge worker, and they have to share workstations for knowledge sharing activities. This can also hamper the knowledge management process as it may slow the process down and it may be inconvenient for staff to share knowledge this way. This often happens in third world countries, where resources are scarce and technology is not as available as in first world countries.

Ease of use of technology is a necessity for quick uptake by users

In any knowledge management programme, the technology used should be configured to be easy to use for the end user to ensure quick uptake. If the technology is hard to understand and not intuitive for the user, it will not be easy to use and the user will not find knowledge management as something that comes naturally to him/her. Specific thought should be given to this in the design process to ensure that knowledge management is not made too complex for the user, but that is made as easy as possible to understand. Technology systems should actually be user tested in the design phase to ensure that ease of use is a feature of the knowledge management systems that will be implemented. This is a very important element due to the fact that many organisations try to implement systems that are too sophisticated for users to understand and work with, and consequently they have no participation in the knowledge management programme. Training is extremely important and people should be sent on refresher courses as often as possible.

Insufficient technology skills can limit staff access to knowledge

Insufficient levels of technology skills can limit staff access to knowledge on platforms such as intranets, communities of practice, etc. Organisations that implement technology for knowledge management purposes, must ensure that staff members are trained to use the systems from a technical point of view. Users must be able to attend training courses where they can learn how to apply the technology to obtain value from knowledge management systems. It is often assumed that staff are more technologically literate than they are, which is an incorrect assumption. When implementing a knowledge management programme, training should not only be given on the principles of knowledge management, but also on the technology that will be used in the programme. Refresher courses should also be given, as technology is updated over time, to ensure that users are kept up to date with changes in software and hardware. If this is not done, the danger is that users may be technologically illiterate and may simply not be able to access critical knowledge and information that they need to do their daily jobs.

Once again, the culture of the organisation, i.e. if the organisation has a high tech culture, can impact the knowledge management culture directly.

Different levels of technology skills can limit staff access to knowledge and can provide challenges in building a knowledge management system

The organisation has to ensure that all staff members have more or less the same level of technology skills in a specific work environment to enable them to access the knowledge management systems. As said above, people need adequate skills to enable them to share their knowledge on technology based forums such as communities of practice and intranets and they need to have similar levels of skills provided to them through organisational training. The organisation needs to enable staff to utilise knowledge management technology in all its forms. Various areas in the organisation will of course require different levels of skills.

Selecting the most applicable hardware and software is crucial to create a knowledge management culture specific to the organisation

When creating a knowledge management programme, it is important to select hardware and software that will blend into the technology environment that already exists in the organisation. This makes user acceptance much easier and ensures that users don't feel that it is another skill that they have to learn, as discussed earlier in this chapter. It will also put less strain on the knowledge management training programme.

It is, however, important to ensure that the technology selected fulfils the purpose that it has been selected to do, and not just because it 'fits the best with the current architecture'. Many organisations buy technology that is not the best option, but fits the best with their current architecture. This is not necessarily the right option for the knowledge management programme, as the organisation may be faced with a number of unanticipated problems down the line. The advantages and disadvantages for the organisation going forward need to be weighed up, alternative routes considered, and the best, practical technology solution should be selected.

Limited understanding of technology value add inhibits the understanding of what knowledge management can do in the organisation

A lack of understanding of the value that technology can add to knowledge management can negatively impact the knowledge management programme in the organisation. Technology within the realm of the knowledge management programme provides a platform for knowledge creation, sharing, harvesting and leveraging. It provides the platforms to create forums such as communities of practice, communities of interest, intranets, and extranets. It allows these forums to have powerful search tools and taxonomies, which makes searching through knowledge and information much easier than before. It also allows people to have access to much more knowledge than they ever had before.

Technology also allows people to share knowledge across organisational and geographical boundaries across the globe, so there is no end to the possibility of reach, of where and with whom they can share knowledge with. Technology has also allowed access to more knowledge which means that people have an ability to learn more and to up-skill themselves in a more controlled manner.

Lack of adherence to set processes with respect to technology undermines the knowledge management organisation

Technology is set up to follow a certain set of processes as set up by the knowledge management team to achieve certain goals and objectives, which in the end is meant to achieve the knowledge management of the organisation.

If these processes are not followed, the value that can be added by technology is also negated. Technology can, e.g. detect who makes submissions to certain communities of practice. If the staff member decides not to fill his/her name in on the submission form, it has a negative impact on the process as the contribution to the knowledge base cannot be measured. It is therefore important that the way that the technology systems are designed and the processes underlying them are followed by staff members, as they have been designed with specific reasons in mind to ensure the efficiency and effectiveness of the knowledge management programme.

Phobia of technology use, e.g. older users

Not all users in organisations are equally comfortable using technology for whatever type of work, including knowledge management. Older people particularly, or people from disadvantaged communities who did not have the privilege of growing up with a computer in the household (such as in third world countries), may have a fear of using technology in their working environment.

They may not understand how to use it, or what value it can add in their specific environment. Therefore knowledge management training is of extreme importance to ensure that staff members receive in-depth training on the use and application of all technology-based systems such as communities of practice and communities of interest, intranets, extranets etc. Users should feel comfortable in using these technologies to enrich their daily working environments. Refresher training is also important, as sometimes not all information can be entrenched in one single session of training.

The courses that pertain to knowledge management technology should be focused on knowledge management and be tailor made to focus on the added value that technology brings to the knowledge management programme. It should be a target to make technology simple to understand and apply, and people should understand the value that it adds.

Organisational structure

The lack of an effective organisational structure for knowledge, e.g. taxonomies

Structuring of knowledge is critical to the success of a knowledge management programme. For knowledge repositories to be meaningful, their structure must reflect the structure of shared mental models or contextual knowledge held tacitly by the business. In most organisations, these structures are neither well defined nor widely shared. Their encoding, is, however, essential for effectively managing explicitly encoded organisational knowledge. This requires an organisation to define what a knowledge unit means and how to meaningfully index and categorise a collection of knowledge units for ease of access, retrieval, exchange, and integration. Knowledge structures lead to easier navigation, organisation and retrieval of knowledge. These structures should be very flexible and must be able to adapt as the business environment changes. They are normally built based on the business process value chain of the organisation. They need to be owned by the knowledge manager and must be kept up to date as the business changes.

No formal recognition of cross-functional capabilities

The knowledge management programme often does not give recognition of staff members' cross-functional capabilities. This is often the cause of silo behaviour created by knowledge not flowing across organisational interdepartmental boundaries. This in turn is often caused by the fact that technology is not available to ensure that this cross-border knowledge flow takes place.

It is important to recognise staff members' cross-functional knowledge capabilities, but that can only be done if technology and knowledge sharing platforms exist, such as communities of practice, communities of interest, and intranets, and are available and transparent to other staff. It ties back to the list of skills that should be available in the organisation in order for people to know what knowledge exists and how that knowledge can be leveraged.

4

Possible ideal solutions for business areas impacting on knowledge management culture

As seen in Chapter 3, there are many organisational culture issues that impact on an organisation's knowledge management culture. These issues can potentially have a negative impact on the knowledge management programme. This chapter will be dedicated to possible ideal solutions for organisational areas that can impact the knowledge management culture in the organisation.

It is helpful to recognise that these solutions exist when designing an organisation's knowledge management programme, to ensure that the programme is implemented successfully from the start.

People related issues

Knowledge and knowledge management is seen as important by the organisation and a premium is placed on it

In the ideal world the organisational culture should encourage knowledge management. It should be seen as an important business initiative in the organisation that is integrated into its day to day operation.

A premium should be placed on the knowledge management lifecycle of creation, sharing, harvesting and leveraging of knowledge and people should readily participate in the knowledge management programme because they can see the value for themselves, their teams and the organisation. The added value of knowledge management should be visible in the business strategy and the execution thereof. The knowledge management programme should be visibly adding value on both a strategic and an operational level, showing alignment between the organisational culture and knowledge management culture.

An internalised knowledge management discipline exists, which is intuitively understood by staff

Ideally, knowledge management is internalised by staff as part of their day to day work and handled as an integrated part of the organisations' business processes. This becomes a discipline according to which staff work from day to day. Knowledge management is not seen as an administrative function, but an integral part of business and the way work is done.

Secondly, knowledge management is not complex to understand and is very intuitive for staff. Not a lot of training should be required and staff would pick up how the systems, processes and rules work intuitively. This is based on the fact that they understand the value knowledge management adds in their daily working environment and how it applies to what they do. They know that the knowledge management lifecycle creates an innovative working environment, where their organisations are at the forefront of major business thinking of the time.

A philosophy of re-use of knowledge should stimulate staff to expand and grow the knowledge base

One of the unique characteristics of knowledge as a commodity is that it can be re-used in different contexts, and have different commercial values in different contexts. Having a philosophy of re-use of knowledge in different contexts should stimulate staff to expand and grow the knowledge base. This potentially increases the monetary value of the organisation's knowledge base.

The more often knowledge is re-used, the more value the organisation generates from the knowledge itself. And the more the knowledge is re-used, the higher the potential of innovation in the organisation. Knowledge as resource will be used effectively and efficiently if re-used.

Employ staff that display new economy behaviours

Employing staff with new economy mindsets is imperative to creating an organisational culture that supports a knowledge management culture. Staff that display new economy mindsets are usually aware of the value of knowledge, as well as the value of technology to mine that knowledge for added value. They understand that knowledge and the knowledge management lifecycle is essential in creating an innovative environment in the organisation where creative thinking and complexity management can take place.

They are astute in utilising knowledge management tools and techniques in their daily work environment. They are usually the gatekeepers of knowledge management in the organisation, and act as points of distribution of where knowledge can be found.

It is therefore essential to build up the right profile of staff in the organisation to change the organisational culture, which in turn will drive the culture towards being a knowledge management culture.

Staff understand that there is more value in sharing knowledge than in hoarding knowledge

In the ideal environment, staff understand that there is more value in sharing knowledge than in hoarding knowledge. They understand that they build their own knowledge as an asset for themselves, to increase their visibility and make themselves more marketable. Staff are therefore happy to share their knowledge with others as it is an 'advertisement' of what they know, and they see this as a positive gesture if others want to use their knowledge. It markets them as thought leaders in their specialist environments. It creates a culture of openness, transparency and innovation around these staff members which is positive for the creation of a knowledge management culture in the organisation (see Figure 9).

Enough trust and transparency exists in the organisation to share and reuse knowledge

As stated before, sharing and re-use of knowledge is crucial in creating a culture of knowledge management in the organisation. However, both trust and transparency are critical to enable the sharing and re-use of knowledge. Without transparency, knowledge cannot really flow throughout the various silos in the organisation. Without trust between people, and between areas in the organisation, knowledge sharing and re-use will also not take place. The ideal knowledge culture requires trust amongst people and

Figure 9 There is more value in sharing knowledge than in hoarding knowledge

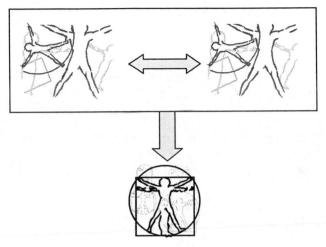

areas in the organisation, together with transparency, which is usually initiated by leaders in the organisation (Parlby and Taylor, 2000). Once again it is clear to see that organisational culture can directly impact on creating a knowledge management culture.

Innovative thought processes are encouraged and rewarded

In the ideal knowledge organisation, innovative thought processes are encouraged and rewarded. Innovation is seen as an outcome of the knowledge management lifecycle (Havens & Knapp, 1999; Gordon & Smith, 2006; Van der Spek & Kingma, 2000). Creation, sharing, harvesting, and leveraging of knowledge lead to innovative thinking and research, which leads to new and innovative solutions. The implementation of these innovative solutions is encouraged and rewarded by the organisation through performance measurement.

Some organisations even have innovation programmes where they formally utilise the knowledge they have to come up with new, innovative solutions in their organisations. These innovations are then logged onto systems, and are evaluated, implemented, and rewarded by management for the best ideas identified. The prevalence of these innovation programmes is growing globally and they are becoming more and more formalised. This shows that organisations understand the value of knowledge and the enrichment thereof into business value.

Willingness to share knowledge between different areas in the organisation

In the ideal knowledge management solution, all areas in the organisation would be willing to share knowledge with each other. There would be no silo knowledge behaviour. There would be transparency from the organisational leadership team, that will facilitate open knowledge flow within the organisation. Transparency will be of the essence and will be filtered down from the highest strategic levels in the organisation to the lowest levels in the organisation. The organisational culture as set up by the leaders of the organisation would thus create an environment in which a knowledge management culture can be built, where knowledge sharing between various areas of the organisation, as well as a knowledge management programme overall, can take place successfully.

Ability to create shared mental models between team members in an organisation

Communities of practice, for example, are ideal vehicles or tools to enable members of a team to create shared mental models of a specific concept. It creates a platform for sharing ideas and knowledge and understanding until concepts are defined and understood, and new working knowledge is created.

The ability to enable the creation of shared mental models is hugely important for new economy thinking in any organisation. Many organisations, due to the lack of knowledge management, have no platforms to create these shared mental models and therefore have no or limited shared references in terms of important business concepts, rules, etc. Having knowledge management in place with its tools that can enable the sharing of mental models is vitally important to think innovatively and to bring innovative solutions to market, and to display new economy thinking.

Diverse and free thinking is encouraged and valued

Diverse and free thinking is encouraged and valued in the ideal knowledge management organisation. This diverse and free thinking has a connection to the concept of innovation, where knowledge flows freely to come up with new business solutions. People are allowed to come up with these solutions, to test them in a controlled environment after being evaluated, and then they are evaluated for efficiency, effectiveness and the positive impact on the organisation.

It thus goes against the grain of a very heavily rules-based business where everything is done according to a preconceived 'recipe'. Although there is management control in the business, there is enough freedom of the mind to create new knowledge, i.e. innovate, to create an environment of free and diverse thinking. Innovation as new economy concept ties in very closely with knowledge management.

Diverse thinking also stimulates creativity and a different base of thinking. Problem resolution, issue and risk handling, and day to day matters can be handled in a more creative, and hopefully more effective and efficient manner. Staff are exposed to different ways of doing the same activity and can see what works the most efficiently. They don't have to do something because it has always been done that way anymore, but because they can now identify it as being the best way of doing it.

Understanding that knowledge management does not function in isolation

In the ideal knowledge management environment, knowledge management does not function in isolation. Firstly, as mentioned before, it is not an administrative function, but a business function that is integrated into the business process value chain of an organisation and is therefore part of the daily work staff members do intuitively. In fact, they do not even realise that they are doing knowledge management.

The second part of understanding that knowledge management does not function in isolation, is realising that it integrates with other specialised areas in the organisation, such as innovation management, eLearning, portals, information management, data mining, customer relationship management, etc. It has a direct impact on certain functions in an organisation that may be absolutely critical. An example would be the following: in any sales environment, it is imperative for the organisation to have a comprehensive profile of the customers they are dealing with to enable e.g. cross-selling and up-selling of products. In the banking environment, for example, the profile of the customer is critical to enable the management of credit risk, and banks use knowledge built up over time about a specific customer to understand the credit risk associated with that customer. In some organisations, knowledge management programmes closely align with, and are sometimes even built from scratch with knowledge management programmes due to their symbiotic relationship.

Some large organisations have also identified complexity management as a discipline within their organisations that needs to be managed. These organisations see a clear link between complexity management and knowledge management in the sense that if the chaos or disorder in the organisation's knowledge base can be sorted out, there will be less complexity for the knowledge worker in his or her working environment, making it less complex to understand the organisational working environment. This will make the staff members more effective and productive as they can access the knowledge they need to do their daily jobs, and they will better understand the environment in which they work (see Figure 10).

| **Figure 10** | **Knowledge does not function in isolation from other disciplines in the organisation** |

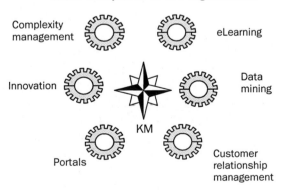

Organisational values and personal values

Trust

In the ideal knowledge management organisation, trust will exist between staff members and all areas or departments within the organisation. Trust is an extremely important element in the world of knowledge management. Without trust, knowledge management activities will not take place.

Trust in organisational terms is usually fostered on a leadership level and cascaded down the hierarchy. The flatter the hierarchy in the organisation, the less the issues around trust there will be. Trust should, however, be a value that the leaders of the organisation instil as a core value in the organisation. The trust will filter through to the knowledge management programme as well, which will then promote knowledge flow amongst staff members in different areas of the organisation. There are two key issues. Firstly there is trust as a leadership value that must be engendered. Secondly, the flatter the hierarchy, the better the chances of trust between staff members.

The organisational culture will thus once again drive the knowledge management culture (see Figure 11).

Respect

Respect for others' knowledge is a very important value in the ideal knowledge management world. Where there is no respect amongst people for each other's knowledge, there will most likely be silo behaviour with respect to knowledge sharing as well as an element of 'knowledge is power' behaviour displayed.

Once again, respect should be an organisational value driven top down from the organisational leadership team

| Figure 11 | Flat organisational hierarchies facilitate an easier and free flow of knowledge |

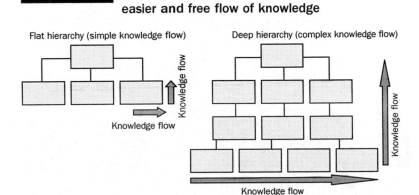

through the organisation. This should cascade through the knowledge management programme. Of course respect can never be enforced, but must be earned by individuals and groups. It is therefore one of the things that must be 'handled with care' because it is not something that can be obtained easily. Once people respect one another, knowledge sharing will take place more readily than before.

Trust and respect are, of course, closely linked. It is very unlikely that someone would respect someone that he or she does not trust, and vice versa. That is also true for that person's knowledge. These values should therefore be engendered in the values of the organisation by the leadership team to enable it to be part of the knowledge management programme.

Trust and respect are two of the most critical elements required with respect to successful implementation of knowledge management. Its importance has not been fully recognised as yet, and therefore organisations are struggling to create their own knowledge management cultures in their organisations. So once again it is clear that the organisational culture and aspects that drive it, ultimately drive the success of the knowledge management implementation.

Recognition

In the ideal knowledge management solution staff members will be recognised for their contributions to the knowledge management programme. The recognition may take different shapes and forms, but their aim will be to energise people to participate in the knowledge management lifecycle.

The recognition may range from monetary recognition, e.g. a bonus or a salary raise, or a prize, or purely a 'thank you' note in the organisation's newsletter.

Recognition is a very important empowerment tool and a tool to encourage people to participate in the knowledge management programme. The key around understanding the role of recognition and the value it presents is that people want to feel valued for the contribution that they make to the knowledge management programme. They want to have their thoughts and their voices heard and recognised in the organisation and be seen as valuable.

Reward

In the ideal knowledge management environment reward for knowledge creation, sharing, harvesting and leveraging is inherent in the way staff work. It is part of the performance measurement system of the organisation. Staff members are measured on whether they take part in the knowledge management programme and are rewarded accordingly via salary increases and promotions. Knowledge management becomes one of the key performance indicators against which they are measured.

Rewards go hand in hand with recognition. People want to be recognised and rewarded for the contribution of intellectual capital that they make towards the knowledge base of the organisation, and also for the way they assist in improving the innovativeness of the organisation through new, creative solution building.

If knowledge is rewarded and recognised, it will also immediately reduce the 'knowledge is power' culture, because it creates a culture of openness and sharing. It therefore assists in shaping a culture of knowledge sharing and knowledge management as a whole.

In the ideal world, the organisation will identify knowledge, and knowledge management activities, as an intangible asset with a value contribution to the organisation which should be measured and rewarded. It will be seen as something with the same value as capital, land or labour and will be rewarded tangibly.

Reciprocation

In the ideal knowledge world, knowledge sharing will be a two-way sharing process between people, where people will never feel hard done by through never receiving their bit of knowledge in the knowledge sharing process. There will always be respect for the other party's knowledge. Reciprocation is a value that is instilled in the organisational culture and is filtered down to the knowledge management programme. It is a value that is set by leadership. It goes hand in hand with transparency in the organisation and the free flow of knowledge. This is once again an example of how the organisational culture influences the knowledge management culture.

Reciprocation will ensure that the 'knowledge is power' mindset is broken and that people freely share their knowledge. It will create greater transparency and a willingness to share knowledge.

Knowledge sharing valued as organisation contribution

Knowledge management, in the ideal context, sees knowledge sharing as a valued contribution to the organisation. Knowledge management is seen as an activity that adds value to the bottom line of the organisation on a day to day basis. Knowledge management is seen as an integral part of the organisation and not as an administrative function. It is integrated in the business process value chain of the organisation and is therefore not something additional that needs to be performed by staff members, but something that is part of their day to day work.

On an individual level, people feel that the knowledge they share with the organisation is valued, and therefore reward and recognition programmes should be implemented for the success of a knowledge management programme. People need to feel that they make a difference in the success of the organisation through their unique contributions, which help the organisation to be strategically more agile and competitive.

Knowledge management and specifically knowledge sharing is valued as a contribution to the organisation as it ensures that knowledge is made explicit and that it can therefore be re-used again in different areas of the organisation, and also in different contexts. Knowledge is thus re-used as an organisational resource to add maximum value.

Knowledge sharing value proposition for the individual

In the perfect knowledge management environment, the individual's value proposition for sharing his or her knowledge will be crystal clear. Staff members will be clear which personal values, as well as values in the organisation, will drive them to share knowledge with others and what the value proposition is for them. Different values drive different individuals, so it may be different for each individual. For some people recognition is a driver, whilst for others monetary rewards are the only drivers that would count. Some people feel that they share knowledge simply because they feel that it is part of doing a good job. There are many drivers that motivate individuals to share knowledge.

To implement knowledge management successfully, however, it is important to understand what the value proposition for individuals is *in a specific organisational environment*, as it is unique to organisations. This needs to be completed during the design phase of the programme, not once the programme has been finally implemented and is running as business as usual. This will ensure that the individuals' value propositions are catered for.

Common goals and a common organisational structure

In the ideal knowledge management world, there will be common organisational goals and a common organisational structure. A flat and uncomplicated common organisational structure will ensure that knowledge flows much more easily throughout the organisation. It also lessens the opportunity for the 'knowledge is power' syndrome, because there are less hierarchical layers in the organisation. The flow of knowledge from staff in top layers in the organisation to staff in bottom layers in the organisation therefore takes place more readily.

Common organisational objectives ensure that processes are aligned and that knowledge that flows within the processes is therefore also aligned. This assists the organisation in reaching its goals and also in implementing its strategy.

It is therefore clear that the organisational structure influences the knowledge management culture of the particular organisation.

Acknowledgement of personal work pride

In the ideal knowledge management world, personal work pride will be acknowledged by the organisation. The organisation will be aware that people take pride in the knowledge and skills that they have accumulated over the years and that they now use in innovative ways to create solutions for the organisation to increase its efficiency and to make it more competitive, and will therefore acknowledge it in some way. The organisation will create a transparent environment where personal work pride and knowledge sharing will be visible and the acknowledgement will be visible as well.

Organisations acknowledge personal work pride in different ways, based upon the organisational culture and the knowledge management culture. Some will acknowledge people's work pride through formal performance measurement systems, whilst others will acknowledge it through recognition in newsletters, or by handing out quarterly prizes, etc. The way the acknowledgement is done depends on the specific culture of the organisation in question.

Measurement

A performance management system will encourage free flow of knowledge and have consequence management for non-participation

The ideal knowledge management solution will provide a performance management system that will encourage free flow of knowledge and have consequence management for non-participation.

The performance management system will have clear measurements within the knowledge management programme for individuals on different levels of the organisation. These measures will be both quantitative and qualitative in nature, and will form part of the performance development programme of the individual across the organisation as a whole. It will encourage staff to participate in the knowledge management programme due to the fact that their promotions and salary increases are dependent on their participation in the knowledge management programme. The performance management will also have consequence management for those who do not participate in the programme.

Performance management will be well entrenched in the ideal knowledge management environment, and will be a cornerstone of enabling a knowledge management culture. Without having performance management, it would be very difficult to create a knowledge management culture.

Once again, it is important that the knowledge management performance management is integrated into the performance management of the organisation, to enforce the concept that knowledge management is an integral part of the business and not an administrative function.

The performance management of individuals will also indicate to the organisation where the gaps in its knowledge base are. This will allow the organisation to improve the knowledge management programme and to improve the alignment between the knowledge management culture and the organisational culture (see Figure 12).

Understanding of the impact of knowledge on all levels of business

The ideal knowledge management solution will display an understanding by all staff members of the impact of knowledge on all levels of the business. Staff members will realise that knowledge management adds value on an operational level, in their day to day work. It assists them with completion of tasks, with decision making, and with research as well as learning and development. They will understand that knowledge management will assist them in building their intellectual capital, which makes them more marketable, and will assist them in working more effectively and efficiently.

Figure 12 **Examples of knowledge management performance measurements**

1. How many contributions did you make to the knowledge base in the past six months?

2. How many training courses did you attend in the past six months?

3. Are you acting as a mentor for someone in the organisation?

4. How many times have you accessed the knowledge base?

5. How do your colleagues rate you in respect of knowledge sharing?

Staff will also realise that knowledge management adds strategic value to the organisation. It assists the organisation to be more agile through quicker decision-making, to improve efficiency and effectiveness, to improve strategic planning, to assist in building and expanding the organisation's business strategy, and to improve the organisation's business process value chain through understanding where the knowledge blockages are and removing them through remedial action.

The organisational culture will impact the knowledge management programme as well as the rest of the business. The organisational culture will determine how well staff members understand the impact of knowledge management on all levels of business. If the organisational culture does not foster knowledge management, it is unlikely that staff will understand the impact of knowledge management on the organisation. If, however, the organisational culture is aligned with the knowledge management culture, it is very likely that the staff will understand the impact that knowledge management has on the organisation and what value it adds.

Ability to show the benefits of knowledge management

In the ideal knowledge management world, the knowledge management programme will have the ability to show the benefits of knowledge management for the organisation. The benefits can be identified quantitatively and qualitatively.

Up to now, most organisations have measured their knowledge management programmes from a qualitative perspective. This is due to the fact that it is very difficult to quantify the value of knowledge, because the value of knowledge changes depending on the context thereof.

The value is also different for different people. It is thus virtually impossible to put a specific monetary value to a specific piece of knowledge at any given time.

In the future, it will hopefully be possible to be able to place an indication of monetary value on knowledge as an organisational asset, in order for it to be measured quantitively over time. This will make it easier to entrench knowledge in the organisation as a strategic asset and staff will be more aware of the value that knowledge adds to the organisation. It is, however, doubtful, that this will ever happen fully. Many authors and scientists over the years have tried to build models to determine the Return On Investment (ROI) of knowledge management, and some of them have gotten some aspects right, but there has not been one overarching model that has worked in the science of knowledge management. This is an area of further discovery that lies ahead, which will provide a great deal of added value to the scientific world.

Strategy and leadership

Implement a business model that supports knowledge management

Implementing a business model that supports knowledge management will be part of the ideal knowledge management environment. Top management will understand the need for integration of knowledge management into the business in a seamless fashion to ensure its success. They will therefore ensure that the way that the programme is set up from the start is done in a strategic way to ensure success.

The organisation ensures that the business process value chain is aligned with the business strategy and business model. Due to the fact that knowledge flows within processes, the knowledge management lifecycle of creation, sharing, harvesting and leveraging will seamlessly integrate with the organisation's business model and strategy. The knowledge management programme will thus not be an administrative function, but a supporting function such as HR, Finance, Procurement, etc., which will assist the core business value chain to be executed effectively and efficiently.

Value, appreciate and acknowledge talent that supports knowledge management behaviour

The ideal knowledge management environment will value, appreciate and acknowledge talent and knowledge that supports knowledge management behaviour.

When recruiting staff, the organisation will look for specific criteria in candidates, e.g. their orientation towards knowledge sharing and creation, their sense of openness and transparency, and their ideas on knowledge management and knowledge management culture specifically. The organisation will thus be oriented towards hiring people with new economy mindsets, whom are innovative and like to work in a learning environment.

The organisation will also value, appreciate and acknowledge talent and knowledge that supports knowledge management behaviour through recognising and rewarding knowledge management contributions that individuals make within the organisation. The organisation will also communicate regularly, as part of its communication function, on knowledge management successes in the organisation to raise the profile of the programme. Awareness will thus be created of knowledge management in the organisation through the human resources and change functions, as well as the knowledge management programme.

Leaders should 'walk the talk' to support new economy leadership principles

In the ideal knowledge management environment leaders should 'walk the talk' to support new economy leadership principles. Leaders will lead by example and participate in the knowledge management programme themselves. They will participate in the activities and processes and will be measured based upon their performance. This creates a precedent for staff to follow.

If leaders do not 'walk the talk', implementing a knowledge management programme will be very difficult, if not impossible. Buy-in from top management is essential for a knowledge management programme to succeed. Integration of knowledge management with, for example, processes, will not happen without the buy-in of leaders of the organisation.

Once again it is clear to see that the organisational culture can have a huge impact on the knowledge management culture. If top management does not buy into the concept of knowledge management and integrate it into the business, the knowledge management programme will not be successful.

Operational issues

Knowledge workers should apply and grow the knowledge base according to their role definition

In the ideal knowledge management environment, knowledge workers apply and grow the knowledge base according to their role definition. Each member of staff has a generic role definition for the daily work that they do, that includes a role definition for knowledge management activities.

The staff members grow the knowledge base and apply the knowledge in it according to their identified roles. This is then measured through their performance development programme, which means the organisation can identify who gatekeepers of knowledge are, who participates in the programme and who doesn't, in which areas of the organisation, etc. This is valuable information to use to build a more robust knowledge management solution going forward, as the organisation understands its strengths, weaknesses, opportunities and threats per role definition via this analysis.

The staff members' search and usage behaviour will also tell the knowledge management programme manager more about the accuracy of the role definitions and whether the knowledge base and its processes, tools and techniques fulfil the needs of the individuals in the organisation. If users are utilising the knowledge management system copiously, the assumption can be made that it does fulfil their needs, but if the usage is low, or declines over time, the organision must assume that it does not fulfil its needs and that something must be done to address that.

Expectations of rate of change vs. actual rate of transformation in the organisation

In the ideal knowledge management environment, expectations of rate of change vs. actual rate of transformation in the organisation will be realistic. Change in any organisation is an activity that takes place slowly, and that is also true for knowledge management, especially as it is a new economy concept. In the ideal world, people's expectations will be managed to understand that the rate of change will most probably be slow, especially in big corporate environments, e.g. pharmaceutical organisations. The truth is that, even in the ideal world, the actual rate of change may actually be extremely slow due to the fact that it is a new economy concept. It is something new for people to get to grips with and to embed into the organisation. Staff should be taken on a journey of understanding the need for knowledge management, the importance thereof in their corporate environment, the value that it adds to their day to day working environment and what strategic and operational benefits it brings to the organisation.

This may sound easy to do, but in a large corporate environment the pace of change is very slow. This can be very disheartening for those trying to implement knowledge management and who are trying to instill a knowledge management culture in the organisation and for those wanting the benefits of the implementation.

It is important to be realistic when embarking on an implementation exercise to understand the organisation's culture in order to understand what the quickest way would be to ensure the uptake of knowledge management, as the organisational culture is often a driver for knowledge management. It is worthwhile to do an organisational culture assessment prior to embarking on a knowledge management journey in order to fit the knowledge management programme to the organisational culture, as it will save the organisation a lot of rework later on in the process.

Supportive environment that allows team based culture and decision making

The ideal knowledge management culture would encourage a supportive environment that allows a team based culture and decision making. The reason for this is to encourage the flow of knowledge and to allow co-creation of solutions in the organisation. This makes the embedding of that knowledge in the business process value chain of the organisation much easier and ensures that acceptance of the solutions by staff members is much quicker.

This type of culture will of course be greatly influenced by the current organisational culture. If the organisation does not have a team based culture, it will be difficult for the knowledge management programme to instill it. It can be done, but it will take more effort and more time.

Processes

Knowledge management is integrated into the organisation's business process value chain

Knowledge always flows within a process, and will therefore always be part of an organisation's business process value chain. Knowledge management by definition will therefore also be part of the organisation's business process value chain. This is crucial, as the business process value chain is one of the core components to enable the organisation's organisational strategy.

This also means that knowledge management is seamlessly integrated into the daily work of staff. It is not a separate entity, but an integrated set of activities that they do as part of the organisation's business process value chain.

The organisation's culture, with respect to implementing and following its own business process value chain, will have a huge impact on the implementation success of knowledge management in the organisation. If the organisation does not adhere to its own business process value chain, knowledge sharing as it is supposed to be done will not take place at all, or it will take place haphazardly. It may even lead to silo knowledge sharing behaviour. The organisational culture will thus impact the knowledge management programme hugely if the linkage between business processes and knowledge flow is not understood well.

Formal knowledge management processes exist

In the ideal knowledge management environment, formal knowledge management processes will exist that will regulate the knowledge management programme. These processes will determine how the lifecycle of knowledge management is executed, from creation, sharing, harvesting, through leveraging of knowledge management. It will also regulate areas in the knowledge management programme, for example the knowledge management strategy implementation.

These knowledge management processes will form part of the organisation's support or enabling processes on the organisation's business process value chain. It will consist of specific activities that are done within the knowledge management programme, e.g. measurement of the usage of the knowledge base, training of staff members on knowledge management, creating new knowledge as innovative ideas for building new business solutions, etc. These processes will be formally mapped and owned by the head of the knowledge management programme.

The processes should be kept up to date by the head of the knowledge management programme as processes change and as the business requirements change. It should therefore be flexible, and be relevant. This is one area where a lot of businesses fail with respect to their knowledge management endeavours.

Once again it can be seen that the organisational culture with respect to how it implements its business process value chain can have a profound effect on the success of the organisation's knowledge management programme.

A comprehensive understanding of all knowledge management processes must exist

In the ideal knowledge management environment, staff members will have a comprehensive understanding of all knowledge management processes. Staff members will have received extensive training on the knowledge management programme, but specifically the knowledge management processes, to ensure that they understand how the programme and processes work, and what is expected of them as participants in the programme.

The availability of training and online help facilities are therefore of the essence in assisting in training knowledge management staff, as well as other staff members, on how knowledge management processes are implemented and executed.

Training updates are also important to ensure that staff keep themselves up to date with changes to the knowledge management programme, and specifically processes, as the business changes over time. This is crucial, as many organisations fail to do this and their programmes are negatively impacted. Processes tend to change quite rapidly over time and should therefore be revisited on a regular basis by the knowledge management programme management manager in the organisation.

Individual accountability exist for knowledge management processes

In the ideal knowledge management programme, individual accountability exists for knowledge management processes.

Staff members in the knowledge management team will have to own the processes to ensure that they are kept relevant and updated, and that they are integrated into the organisational business process value chain. This is extremely important because without ownership, processes will be neglected, which will impact the whole knowledge management programme negatively.

Technology and other channels

Available funds for knowledge management technology developments

Availability of funds for technology developments will not be an issue in the ideal knowledge management environment. This is extremely important as technology is a vital component of a knowledge management programme. Technology used for knowledge management will fit into the architecture of the organisation and will integrate seamlessly into current applications. This means that current knowledge will be available via the knowledge management technology based system, e.g. intranet, communities of practice, etc.

Although technology can be very costly, it has to be born in mind that it is a crucial vehicle to break down silo behaviour in terms of knowledge flow and sharing. It is also a vehicle that acts as the corporate memory for the organisation's knowledge base, and therefore adequate funds must be made available.

Technology is also a crucial vehicle to enhance the accessibility of knowledge through search tools, and therefore the benefit of using the technology outweighs the cost of the hardware. Through more efficient access to the knowledge base, the organisation can make quicker and more efficient decisions, and therefore be more agile in the market. Response to changes in the marketplace can be more effective.

The choice of the organisation's technology architecture team and their perceptions towards knowledge management, and what they understand knowledge management to be, will have a critical impact on the knowledge management programme. If inappropriate technology is selected for knowledge management activities, the knowledge management programme will be negatively impacted. For example, in many organisations, the technology architecture team starts out by creating a shared file structure scheme to store shared files. At first this works well, until there are so many documents that nobody can find anything and it becomes unmanageable. It is therefore crucial that the knowledge management team should have a strong role to play in selecting the required knowledge management technology.

Intuitive use of technology for knowledge management

Intuitive use of technology is critical for the ideal knowledge management environment. Technology should be easy to use and understand, and should not require hours of training. The easiest way to achieve this is to select technology that is already being used in the organisation, if possible. If this is not possible, then staff members need to be trained and after training they need to pick up the use of the technology very quickly and effectively. It is important to note that the way an organisation implements its technology can have a vast impact on the successful implementation of a knowledge management programme.

The design of the knowledge base is therefore of great importance. It is the responsibility of the knowledge management programme to ensure that the knowledge base design is not too complex. From a technological perspective it must be intuitive to use. Users of the system must also receive training on the knowledge base and how it works, as well as on how the technology side works. Training manuals must be provided by the knowledge management team.

Technology literacy on all levels

In the ideal knowledge management environment, technology literacy should exist on all levels. Adequate training is provided to all levels of staff in order for them to be able to utilise the knowledge management system to the fullest. It is important that the most junior person must be able to work on the knowledge management system, but also the most senior executive. It is often found that the senior executives do not have time to attend training to learn how to use the knowledge management system. They get staff to help them to obtain knowledge from the system as and when they need to.

This, however, presents many problems, e.g. from a buy-in perspective, from a leadership perspective, from a culture creation perspective, etc. It is therefore very important for executives to make time in their busy schedules to be trained on how to use the technology-based knowledge management system. A lot of the success of the whole knowledge management programme depends on 'walking the talk'.

Once again it is evident that the organisational culture or orientation towards something as simple as computer training can influence the successful implementation of a knowledge management programme.

Availability of the knowledge management system 24/7 through a single point of access

Availability of the knowledge management system 24/7 from remote sites through a single point of entry will be possible in the ideal knowledge management environment. This means effectively that staff members will be able to access their organisation's knowledge base from any location, at any time of day or night.

This is an important feature of the knowledge management programme, as people are working in a virtual world now and therefore these facilities are of the essence to ensure a new economy organisation. Staff members must be enabled to work from wherever they are located. They should have access through one single point of access to the knowledge base, meaning that they do not have to search in multiple databases for knowledge. The search for organisational knowledge must be made simple and effective for staff members of new economy organisations.

This will leave the organisation and its staff members in a place where it can be more agile due to quicker and more effective decision making. The organisation will also have an understanding of what knowledge resources are available in the organisation, as knowledge of it will all be available through one single point of entry.

Once again, through the provision of the right infrastructure and a culture of centralisation, the organisational culture can have a huge impact on the knowledge management programme.

User requirements are an important decision making factor in vendor selection

In the ideal knowledge management environment, user requirements are an important decision making factor in vendor selection with respect to technology. From a knowledge management programme point of view, it is extremely important that user requirements are taken into account when undertaking a vendor selection for a knowledge management programme. In many organisations, it is the case that the IT Department dictates what shall be used. This is clearly the incorrect approach to follow as they do not necessarily understand the needs and requirements of the knowledge management users.

The knowledge management programme manager must therefore ensure that an in-depth user requirement study is made to enable his/her team to assess which vendor will be the most appropriate to utilise for the knowledge management programme going forward. This must then be discussed with the IT department and the most appropriate hardware and software must be selected, based on the user requirements and the organisation's architecture.

Organisational structure

A single point of entry to all knowledge in the organisation exists

In the ideal knowledge management environment, a single point of entry will exist, e.g. through an intranet. This means that all knowledge stores, communities of practice, communities of interest, and centres of excellence will be accessible in one location. It will make it easy for the user to access, as he/she will only have to search in one location. It also provides one integrated 'working environment' for staff where they know they can get their knowledge and information from, so it is an integrated part of their day to day working life.

Clear knowledge domains have been defined in the organisation

Finally, in the ideal knowledge management environment clear knowledge management domains are defined in a taxonomy. A taxonomy is the structure of the knowledge base. It assists staff members in navigating the knowledge base in a structured way via various domains and sub-domains as identified by the organisation. Taxonomies will differ from organisation to organisation as they are based upon the business process value chain of the organisation, so there is no blueprint on how to build a taxonomy.

Having a taxonomy as part of the knowledge management programme in the organisation is, however, absolutely critical to the success of the programme. The organisational culture can have a definitive impact here. If domains are not clearly defined, it will be very difficult to define a taxonomy, which will negatively impact the knowledge management programme, and vice versa.

5

A model to identify and manage knowledge management culture issues in organisations

The model is a practical model oriented towards both the strategic and operational parts of the organisation. The model identifies a number of components and asks a number of questions on key issues around the organisation's knowledge management culture itself, keeping the impact of organisational culture, as discussed above, in mind.

The model will provide a framework against which knowledge management can be safely implemented, knowing that the most important issues have been thought of and have been covered. This is not to say that problems and new issues won't crop up that are not addressed by this model. Knowledge management as a discipline is growing at such an exponential rate that it is hard to keep up with developments as they happen.

Strategic knowledge management cultural issues

Strategic knowledge management cultural issues are critical to the success of the knowledge management programme and should be attended to in detail. This is not an exercise that should be done as a quick, easy effort, but time should be taken to do this in great detail to ensure that it is done as correctly as possible. This will form the foundation of the knowledge management programme going forward and is therefore of the utmost importance. This is also a way where the knowledge management programme can be used to influence the organisational culture, rather than let the organisational culture dictate the knowledge management culture (see Figure 13).

Knowledge management definition

Knowledge management needs to be defined in the organisational context due to the fact that knowledge management means different things to different people. To ensure a common understanding amongst staff members, it

Figure 13 Strategic knowledge management cultural issues

Strategic knowledge management issues

- Knowledge management definition
- Knowledge management drivers
- Knowledge management model
- Knowledge management vision
- Knowledge management goals
- Knowledge management objectives
- Values to be instilled to make knowledge management successful
- Knowledge management critical success factors
- Knowledge management barriers
- Knowledge management value proposition

- Knowledge management governance, roles and responsibilities
- Knowledge management risks and interdependencies
- Knowledge management stakeholders
- Knowledge management measures of success
- Knowledge management guiding principles and assumptions
- Knowledge management gatekeepers
- Organisational culture
- Financials
- Technology landscape
- Knowledge management roadmap

is important to define a customised knowledge management definition for the organisation.

This definition has to be signed off by the knowledge management team. It then needs to be presented to and get some form of buy-in from top management in the organisation to ensure that they fully understand what knowledge management is, and that they will be happy to promulgate it in the organisation.

Once buy-in has been obtained, a knowledge management charter must be compiled. The charter must be started by including the definition of knowledge in the context of the organisation, as this will be the point of departure of the knowledge management programme.

The knowledge management programme manager must then ensure that a communication plan is put together to ensure that employees start to understand the concept of knowledge management.

Once the process has been followed, it is always good to obtain feedback from staff members on what they think of the concept and what they think needs to change. This will ensure that when embarking on a large knowledge management programme, it is taken into account what the overall programme is perceived to be and it can be adapted accordingly in order for user acceptance to be higher.

Once feedback has been adopted and the charter is ready for use, the knowledge management programme is ready to move onto the next phase.

Knowledge management drivers

It is essential to determine what the drivers are for knowledge management in the organisation. Drivers for knowledge management will differ from organisation to organisation. If the knowledge management programme manager does not understand the drivers of knowledge management, it will be very difficult to effectively and efficiently implement knowledge management in the organisation, as the person will not know what to address, or what the 'hot spots' are that need specific attention. (Du Plessis, 2005).

One of the first drivers in today's economy is that knowledge is recognised as a commodity in the knowledge economy. Managers will increasingly be judged by how they add value to the organisation by retaining and increasing the capital implicit in their customer base, infrastructure and people. As much executive attention should be placed on managing intellectual capital as should be on managing human capital, land, etc.

Knowledge is seen as a commodity that can lead to competitive advantage. It therefore necessitates being managed as such to derive the most value from it through adequate 'leverage. Knowledge is many organisations' product, e.g. management consultancies. Due to the fact that knowledge is seen as an organisational commodity, protection against external leakage of organisational knowledge is a driver for knowledge management.

Knowledge attrition is also a driver for knowledge management. Employees change jobs more readily in today's working environment. When they leave, they take their knowledge and experience with them, leading to knowledge attrition for the organisation. Organisations are now focusing on managing the knowledge through knowledge management programmes and systems, rather than getting employees to stay with the organisation.

Knowledge is a necessary and sustainable source of competitive advantage. In an era characterised by uncertainty, organisations that consistently create new knowledge, disseminate it to all in the organisation and build it into products and services, can be considered to be competitive and innovative. Knowledge provides the organisation with a competitive advantage as it allows the organisation to solve problems and seize opportunities in the market as quickly as possible.

Another driver is that knowledge management contributes to more effective decision-making. Decisions in today's world are taken in short timeframes with more knowledge at hand than ever before. Strategic decision making depends on predicting what competitors will do. The ability to predict is one of the bases of innovation. Decision making performance may be impacted, because the best know-how is not available to those making the decisions when and where it is needed. Many organisations are implementing knowledge management to ensure that these decision makers have adequate and accurate knowledge at their fingertips to ensure good quality decision-making.

Another driver for knowledge management is the Internet, improved telecommunications, and technology. Customers generate a wealth of information and knowledge as they move around the Internet. Organisations are driven to implement knowledge management in order to harvest, organise, analyse and leverage this knowledge. Dramatic changes in the way of working and developments in telecommunications and technology have made knowledge management increasingly important. This leads to a requirement for organisations to manage the wealth of knowledge that is travelling through these high-speed networks and telecommunications technologies.

Collaboration as driver for knowledge management is increasing, necessitating platforms for collaboration and knowledge sharing across geographical and organisational boundaries. Organisations are compelled to implement knowledge management to enable the creation of platforms, processes and standards for collaboration and knowledge sharing across geographical and organisational boundaries.

Another driver for knowledge management is organisational and geographical distribution. Organisations are increasingly working in a distributed environment. Knowledge is often fragmented within the organisation. Without knowledge management, knowledge sharing is not effective, mostly taking place in areas that are closest to one another in terms of physical proximity. Organisations implement knowledge management to facilitate the creation, sharing, harvesting and leveraging of knowledge across geographical as well as organisational boundaries.

Overcoming internal inefficiencies is a driver for knowledge management. Organisations are concerned with how experience can be transferred more effectively and quickly and how to capture and document valuable insight so that it can be reused. Missed opportunities, wasted time and operational inefficiencies represent competitive disadvantage and contribute to excessive cost, reduced revenue and poor bottom line. This is why organisations implement knowledge management.

Time and cost savings are also drivers for knowledge management. People find it difficult to know what knowledge is available and which sources are the best to use. This means they waste time in finding the right sources. Time saving, and therefore also a cost saving, is achieved in terms of prevention of duplication of work due to the knowledge of what knowledge already exists, or what work has been done before. Reusing knowledge in different contexts creates new insights in the organisation. The reuse of the knowledge increases the scope and value of the knowledge.

An important driver for knowledge management is to ensure knowledge is not hoarded, but is able to flow through the organisation in order for it to be available to everyone. Knowledge hoarding takes place due to the 'knowledge is power' syndrome in most organisations. Hoarding often also takes place within functional silos in the organisation or where competition exists between various business units.

Knowledge management can assist in overcoming this barrier through rewarding people for sharing their knowledge. People also often hoard knowledge because no proper platforms exist to enable them to share their knowledge effectively. Knowledge management can provide these knowledge-sharing platforms. (Du Plessis, 2005).

Knowledge management model

A knowledge management model depicting the way that knowledge management will be implemented and operationalised in the organisation must be drawn up as part of the knowledge management programme. The knowledge management model is a visual representation of the knowledge management definition, vision and drivers and will clearly show what will be implemented, how it will be implemented, how it will be operationalised and what the potential outcome will be.

A knowledge management model is an essential part of any knowledge management programme and in creating a knowledge management culture in the organisation. The visual representation assists in embedding the culture of what the programme is aiming to achieve and it is always a beacon to refer back to when setting up communication programmes, as well as culture and awareness creation programmes.

It is important that the model is not cast in stone, but is a living model and that it is adjustable as the organisation grows. Knowledge management is a growing discipline and changes as the organisation changes, and therefore the model will also need to be adaptable as the organisation changes.

The model is owned by the knowledge management programme, but should be co-created with staff members in the organisation. This is extremely important to ensure buy-in and quick uptake into the organisational culture once implemented. It is important to understand knowledge management from the user's point of view and to ensure that the model that will be implemented is one that is acceptable to them with respect to the daily challenges they face regarding knowledge management. It is also important that the actual visual representation is signed off by the staff members or users, because it makes buy-in and user take-up later on in the process much easier.

Knowledge management vision

Once knowledge management has been finalised, a vision for knowledge management should be defined. A vision can be defined as an idea or a mental picture of what the end state of the knowledge management programme should look like. The vision should be a short, concise statement that summarises what the essence of the knowledge management programme will entail.

The vision should be shared with both the leadership of the organisation as well as the general staff to ensure buy-in. This can be done via a communication plan drawn up by the knowledge management programme manager. Staff and leaders should be given a chance to give feedback on the vision in order to ensure that the final version of the vision is a co-created one. That will ensure buy-in and quicker user adoption.

The vision is important with respect to the knowledge management programme because, firstly, it gives direction, and secondly, provides focus to the programmme, which will drive performance to enable change in the future.

Once the vision has been finalised and accepted by the organisation, it must be communicated on a continuous basis using various marketing channels, such as newsletters, e-mails, TV broadcasts, radio broadcasts, intranet articles, etc. It is imperative that this message keeps its momentum for an adequate length of time through to the implementation period, as this is the lynchpin of the programme going forward.

It is the responsibility of the knowledge management programme manager and his/her team to ensure that this happens smoothly in the organisation.

Knowledge management goals

Once the organisation has defined its knowledge management definition and the knowledge management model that it wants to implement, it needs to clearly identify its top two or three goals that it wants to achieve with the knowledge management programme. A goal can be defined as a purpose at which an endeavour can be directed, so the goals would be defining the result that the organisation would like to achieve via the knowledge management programme.

The goals would provide direction to the knowledge management programme, providing it with some scope and focus for the programme. The goals are therefore very important, as they will be directly dictating the culture of the knowledge management programme and therefore of the organisation.

Once again it is important that these goals are co-created with staff members in the business to ensure quicker user uptake later on when the programme is implemented. Co-creation creates a greater feeling of ownership than if the knowledge management team create these goals in isolation and just communicate them to the business. Co-creation is also the first step in breaking down silo behaviour with respect to knowledge creation and knowledge sharing in the knowledge management programme.

Knowledge management objectives

Once the knowledge management programme's goals have been identified and finalised, then the knowledge management programme objectives that will be used to fulfil these goals must be defined. Objectives can be defined as statements describing the results to be achieved by a programme, and the manner in which these results will be achieved over a specified period of time. Usually, objectives are linked to one or more programme goals. The objectives will provide a more concrete means of showing how the goals will be met and how the knowledge management programme will be rolled out within the organisation.

The objectives should also be co-created with staff members in order to ensure quicker uptake later on and to ensure a feeling of ownership by the business. They will provide clarity on what activities will be done specifically in the knowledge management programme and what they hope to achieve. They should also indicate who will be responsible for achieving which objectives.

The knowledge management objectives should be clearly aligned with the knowledge management goals and, in turn, should be aligned with the business strategy of the organisation if the knowledge management programme wants to be embedded into the day to day business of the organisation. This is extremely important, because if this is not done at this juncture, knowledge management will just fall into the trap of being an administrative function in the business, and therefore not integrated into the business process value chain and not integrated with the organisational strategy.

Values to be instilled to make knowledge management successful

This is probably one of the most difficult sections to write about, because it can differ vastly from one organisation to another. However, over many years of practice, some common values repeatedly come to the fore in organisations that are prerequisites with respect to successful knowledge management implementations.

The first value is that the value of the knowledge management lifecycle, i.e. creation, sharing, harvesting, and leveraging lies with the individual, and only thereafter with the team and/or the organisation. Knowledge management is an individually oriented activity which is turned into a group activity. Hence the great need for reward and recognition on an individual level. People want to be recognised for their contribution to the organisation's knowledge management lifecycle, whether in a team or in a group. People want to have their personal pride respected with respect to the work that they do and the contributions they deliver. It sounds like an antithesis as knowledge management is really built on teamwork and team participation, but the individual's participation must be recognised first for the programme to be successful.

Staff members must also feel that there is an individual value proposition for sharing knowledge or participating in the knowledge management lifecycle. Once again this comes back to reward and recognition – staff members want to be valued for what they know and be rewarded and recognised for it. What the reward or recognition entails will differ from organisation to organisation.

It is also important that the organisation has a culture of transparency, openness and trust. Without these three basic values, knowledge flow throughout the organisation will be difficult. It will be difficult between different hierarchies, but also between different areas in the organisation, e.g. different departments. Often these three values are dictated by the organisational culture rather than the knowledge management programmme. It can, however, present endless hassles for the knowledge management programme and even make it fail. These three values are therefore extremely important to the knowledge management programme.

Staff members must also feel that learning is seen as a value and a learning culture must be created in the organisation if a knowledge management programme is to succeed. Self-learning should be incentivised and staff should want to participate in this learning culture out of their own free will. This should also greatly assist in creating a culture of cross-skilling, where people can cross-skill themselves in a learning environment and widen their world of learning and of working opportunities. This provides instantaneous value to the knowledge management programme.

Finally, staff must feel that, with respect to values and the knowledge management programme, there are common goals and a common culture. This is vital to make the programme work. The model that is outlined in this chapter is, therefore, so important, as it is the first step in getting to the common goals and common culture that a knowledge management programme needs.

Knowledge management critical success factors

Identifying knowledge management critical success factors for the knowledge management programme is essential for successful implementation of the programme. The critical successful factors will tell the story of what will make or break the programme, or where the biggest pitfalls will be found.

It is the responsibility of the knowledge management programme manager to determine what these critical success factors are. Many of these critical success factors are often determined by the organisational culture, as explained in earlier chapters, and may therefore be difficult and slow to change. Others may be part and parcel of the knowledge management programme itself and may therefore be easier to change.

There are also different ways to determine what these critical success factors are. Once again, involvement of staff in determining what these factors are is of the essence. Interviews, questionnaires, facilitated work sessions and feedback through general mechanisms such as an intranet are all ways that can be used to determine what the critical success factors may be in a specific organisation. Once again it is important to note that critical success factors will differ from one organisation to the next, so there is no blueprint that one can work from here. These critical success factors will be unique to each organisation. The way in which each of these critical success factors are addressed will also be unique, depending on the circumstances in the organisation and the organisational culture.

Knowledge management barriers

The next important issue is to determine what barriers can be identified in the organisation that can negatively impact the implementation and operation of knowledge management in the organisation. This is the responsibility of the knowledge management programme manger and his or her team together with staff members, as the barriers will most likely be integrated in the day to day activities of the staff members. They would be most likely to know what the barriers to knowledge management are.

It is vital that these barriers are identified, as this will impact the knowledge management lifecycle on all levels. If the knowledge management programme has no idea what the barriers of knowledge management are, it is going to be very difficult to put measures in place to rectify the situation and to get the knowledge management lifecycle working in balance again.

Once the barriers have been identified, the knowledge management programme manager should categorise the barriers into the areas of the knowledge management lifecycle, namely create, share, harvest and leverage to identify where the main bottlenecks of knowledge management lie within the organisation. Doing it this way also makes it easier to see if the barriers are all in one area of the knowledge management lifecycle, which often happens. Plans of action then need to be put into place to address the barriers in each of these areas to ensure that the issues are addressed. Measurements also need to be put into place to determine if the plans that have been put into place are actually successful over a period of time. If not, alternative solutions should be considered.

Knowledge management value proposition

The knowledge management programme management team should very clearly define the knowledge management value proposition for the organisation. The value proposition should be clear, concise and measurable. It should be clearly understood by individuals in the organisation and the formulated value proposition should show the value of knowledge management in the organisation for both the individual as well as the organisation. Once again, co-creation with the staff will ensure bigger buy-in and quicker uptake later on in the implementation phase.

The value proposition is immensely important for the knowledge management programme to succeed as discussed in previous chapters. Staff members want to see the value of participation in the knowledge management lifecycle and how they will be recognised and rewarded for their efforts. They also want to see and understand how it will benefit the organisation and what positive impact it will have. It is therefore of critical importance that the knowledge management programme manager must not only be able to communicate this to the organisation as a whole, but also in his or her communication messages speak to the heart of the individuals working in the organisation, in order to show the value of individual contributions.

This is probably one of the most difficult areas of the knowledge management programme to get right. The knowledge management value proposition is often highly influenced by the organisational culture, and often that influence is negative. This makes it very difficult to try and implement knowledge management from a positive perspective and to try and create a positive climate and culture for knowledge management to thrive in. It is therefore very important for knowledge management to be an integrated part of the business, in order for it to have more leverage with respect to the impact that it can have to effect change in the organisation when required. If knowledge management is integrated into the business process value chain and into the business functions, it will be much easier to communicate the knowledge management value proposition and to gain acceptance for it by the staff members.

Knowledge management governance and roles and responsibilities

In the knowledge management programme structure, governance is very important. Roles and responsibilities as well as governance-related activities are crucial to ensure that knowledge management as a programme is run professionally and gets the attention from the organisational management team that it deserves.

It is the role of the organisation's Human Resources team to provide the role profile of the knowledge management programme manager. Thereafter, it is the role of the knowledge management programme manager to select his or her team for the implementation of the knowledge management solution as well as for running the operational side of the programme. The programme manager is responsible for clarifying each person's roles and responsibilities through a clear performance development programme as prescribed by the Human Resources division of the organisation. A proper reporting structure should be put in place to ensure that reporting lines and roles and responsibilities are clear not only within the team, but also within the organisation. A performance development plan needs to be developed with each of the team members, as with all staff members in the organisation.

It is extremely important from a governance perspective for the knowledge management programme manager to identify who the internal stakeholders of the knowledge manage management programme in the organisation are. A governance structure must be set up to ensure that there is adequate stakeholder management between the knowledge management programme manager and his/her team and the stakeholders and to ensure that the organisation's governance is being followed.

Knowledge management risks and interdependencies

Once the organisation's value proposition has been defined, it is important to identify any risks and interdependencies that the implementation of a knowledge management programme may bring to the organisation and the organisational culture. It is therefore, as stated in previous chapters, important to understand the organisational culture prior to embarking on a knowledge management implementation.

In identifying risks and interdependencies, the involvement of staff is crucial. They work at the 'coal face' every day and will be in the best position to know what the real risks and interdependencies are, and therefore their involvement is critical. Risks and interdependencies may be identified in a variety of ways. Interviews, focus groups, communities of interest, discussion forums and a feedback mechanism, e.g. an e-mail address on an intranet may be ways of gathering information on what staff perceive as possible risks and interdependencies. Staff may also be prompted with specific risks and interdependencies that they may not have thought of as valid in a particular scenario.

Once the risks and interdependencies have been identified, the knowledge management programme manager needs to set up an action plan for managing these risks. Names need to be allocated to each risk, with a mitigating action as to how the risk will be resolved and by which date. Interdependencies must also be monitored by specific people allocated to the tasks. These people must give regular feedback to the knowledge management progamme manager on the impact of the interdependencies on the knowledge management programme and other areas of the business in order for the required action to be taken.

Knowledge management stakeholders

When implementing a knowledge management programme, identifying internal as well as external stakeholders is very important, as they are vehicles in establishing the programme in the organisation.

A stakeholder can be defined as any party that may have a significant impact on the implementation and/or operation of the programme. An example of an internal stakeholder is the IT department, as they will be responsible for creating IT platforms for knowledge sharing. An example of an external stakeholder is a provider of industry information, such as an information provider. Once the list of stakeholders have been drawn up by the knowledge management team, a communication plan has to be drawn up to engage with the stakeholders on a regular basis to ensure that they are aware of what is happening within the knowledge management programme, where the programme is at, what impact their role will have and when their involvement will be required. It is extremely important to take these people on the journey with the team, or else the team may be faced with all sorts of obstacles, e.g. stakeholders not understanding their roles and the impact it may have on the knowledge management programme. Many stakeholders have an indirect impact, which makes it very important to keep them with the programme and understanding where it is at. This is the same for internal as well as external stakeholders.

The stakeholder map is a very important tool for the knowledge management programme and needs to be tied to specific roles and responsibilities within the team. It has to be revisited on a regular basis to ensure stakeholder buy-in is kept at an optimum level.

Knowledge management measures of success

Whilst having all these wonderful tools in place when implementing a knowledge management programme is a great help, at the end of it all one has to be able to measure if is functioning successfully. Therefore it is important for the knowledge management team to identify measures of success for the organisation's knowledge management programme.

Once again, these measures of success will differ from organisation to organisation, depending on the specific programme. It is, however, important to know how the organisation will know that its programme is successful.

The knowledge management team will most probably come up with the greatest majority of measurements. It should be added though, that it may be worthwhile once again to involve staff members and hear what their ideas are around this. They sometimes come up with very interesting and good ideas around these issues and can add valuable contributions. This is a difficult exercise and as many heads as possible should be used to determine these measures.

The measures of success should also be relayed back to the staff members by the knowledge management programme manager in a communication to show how serious the team is in making knowledge management successful in the organisation. It keeps levels of interest high and shows the programme's level of dedication to the organisation and the contribution thereof to staff members. It also creates visibility in the organisation.

Knowledge management guiding principles and assumptions

As with any programme implementation in an organisation, a knowledge management programme implementation will work with some guiding principles and assumptions. The reason for this is that the environment in which the implementation will take place is not one hundred percent clear and therefore many unknowns exist. To this end, assumptions sometimes have to be made and guiding principles have to be used to enable the finalisation of the design, the implementation, etc.

This is not unusual for a programme like this. However, the less guiding principles and assumptions can be used and the more firm understanding can be had of the implementation environment, the better. It creates a more stable environment for the future and less rework that has to be done at a later stage. It also minimises risk in working in an unknown environment.

Knowledge management gatekeepers

When implementing a knowledge management programme, it is important to know who the knowledge management gatekeepers in the organisation are. Knowledge management gatekeepers are those staff members who are usually either thought leaders in the organisation, or alternatively know a lot on how the knowledge management lifecycle operates in the organisation, especially how knowledge flows in the organisation.

Gatekeepers should be used in the knowledge management implementation as they can be used as anchor points for spreading the message about the knowledge management implementation, obtaining buy-in from other staff members and for train-the-trainer purposes. They can be used very effectively to effect any change that is required within the knowledge management programme. They can also be used to unblock blockages in the flow of knowledge identified in the organisation, which can be very useful later on once the programme is in its operational phase.

Organisational culture

As pointed out in the chapters above, and as stated in the topic of this book, it is essential to understand the organisational culture of an organisation to some extent *prior* to embarking on a knowledge management implementation, as the organisational culture will have a very definitive impact on the culture of the knowledge management programme. Without understanding some of the subtleties of the culture of the organisation, the knowledge management programme may fail dismally.

There is no knowledge management blueprint that one can follow for implementations exactly for this one reason – organisational cultures differ and therefore the solutions that are implemented will differ. It is thus very important to understand the environment and the culture that the knowledge management implementation is going to take place in, to ensure that it will be successful.

There are numerous ways to go about doing this. The knowledge management team can use previous culture studies that have been performed by e.g. the Human Resources division in the organisation. They can thus draw upon previous work that has been done in this environment. The team may also decide to do a small organisational culture 'dipstick' questionnaire themselves in the organisation with the help of Human Resources.

Once the knowledge management team has worked through the information they get via these sources, they will be in a much better position to know what to implement, how to implement it, where to implement it and who should be involved. The knowledge management team can then start their planning and design, based on more solid facts around the organisation itself, rather than building a solution in a vacuum without understanding the impact of people and culture and what they bring to the organisation.

Financials

When embarking on a knowledge management programme, it is important to understand the financial impact it will have on the organisation. The knowledge management programme manager should, subsequent to the programme design, provide a financial impact summary to the top management team of the organisation of the initial setup cost as well as the operational cost going forward. The financials should be detailed with respect to e.g. technology costs, people costs, training costs, infrastructure costs, and process costs.

Together with the costs that the knowledge management programme will hold for the organisation, the benefits should also be indicated to the top management team. A cost benefit assessment will allow the top management team to make more informed decisions.

The organisational culture regarding spending will have a huge impact on spending on programmes like knowledge management. It is therefore important to understand what the organisation's culture is in this regard, and tailor the financials to best suit the culture of the organisation, to ensure that the knowledge management programme is awarded the most possible finances as possible.

The knowledge management programme manager should then set up a proper financial budget for the knowledge management programme, both for set-up and for operations. Financial management is also critical to the success of a knowledge management programme.

Technology landscape

When implementing a knowledge management programme, identifying the technology landscape is quite a complex task. Firstly, the technology that is essential for the knowledge management programme needs to be identified. This then needs to be mapped to the current organisational technology architecture in the organisation to determine the architectural fit. If there is a discrepancy in the technological fit, decisions need to be made whether the knowledge management technology will be accommodated, or whether the current technology in the organisation will be used and adapted to fit the knowledge management programme's needs.

This is a very critical and very difficult decision to make, and is often not in the hands of the knowledge management programme manager to make. The knowledge management programme manager can influence the decision, but once again in most organisations the organisational structures will weigh stronger than the need of just one programme. It may therefore be prudent to, at the outset of investigations, look at what technology is available in the organisation that can be used effectively in the knowledge management programme, and only then start looking externally at other products. This will minimise the decision making effort and will make the process less complex.

Technology is, however, an important part of the knowledge management programme and the team should put adequate time and effort into planning the technology landscape going forward.

Knowledge management roadmap

The knowledge management roadmap for implementation is crucial to ensure that everyone has a clear understanding on how the knowledge management programme will be implemented. The knowledge management team should co-create this knowledge management roadmap with members of staff to determine in which areas of the organisation to start the implementation and where they should proceed to from there. Co-creation is a key factor in this activity to ensure buy-in from staff members and to create awareness of the implementation and what it will entail.

The roadmap of the knowledge management programme should be drawn up subsequent to the co-creation with the staff members and played back to them for buy-in and agreement. It should then be presented by the knowledge management programme manager to the organisational top management team to ensure that the timing and the sequence of implementation is suitable for the organisation with respect to other initiatives that may be running at that time. If the top management is not satisfied, the roadmap will have to be adjusted. This happens quite often, as there are so many initiatives running in an organisation at one time that it is sometimes difficult to keep track of all of them and the impact it would have to roll them out in parallel at a given time.

The roadmap is then reworked until accepted for implementation by top management. The knowledge management programme management team can then go ahead with the implementation kick-off activities.

Operational knowledge management cultural Issues

Operational knowledge management cultural issues are also critical to the success of the knowledge management programme. On the operational level, the knowledge management issues will differ from organisation to organisation even more than on the strategic level. The uniqueness will be clearly evident.

However, it is of the utmost importance to understand which of the operational cultural issues have an impact on the knowledge management programme and how that can be addressed. Once again, this is also a way where the knowledge management programme can be used to influence the organisational culture, rather than let the organisational culture dictate the knowledge management culture.

In any organisation, knowledge management takes place. How formalised or non-formalised it is, is debatable. Just as the knowledge management team needs to understand the organisational culture before they embark on a knowledge management programme, they need to understand to what extent knowledge management takes place in the organisation or not. The framework below is aimed at providing some issues that need to be highlighted to identify the state of knowledge management in the organisation. It is a general framework and can be adapted to suit the organisation.

People issues

Focus group/community activities

The first question that should be asked is whether focus group or any other community activity exists where knowledge is shared. Once it is established that there are communities that exist, it should be probed what the aim of these communities are, how regularly they meet, and how they go about creating and sharing knowledge, as well as how they leverage knowledge within the community. It is also important to determine what value the community adds, to whom and why. This will give the knowledge management team a better understanding of what community activity already takes place prior to designing a knowledge management programme, and will provide ideas on what is successful and what the culture of the organisation is like with respect to the knowledge management lifecycle. It will provide valuable input in successfully designing knowledge management communities within the knowledge management programme.

If the knowledge management team finds that there is very little community activity with very little knowledge sharing taking place, this is a very important finding. It means that the knowledge flow in the organisation is very limited, that communities as cultural entities do not exist in the organisation and are also not part of the knowledge management environment. This means that in the design of a knowledge management programme, strong emphasis should be put on implementing e.g. communities of practice as a means of creating and sharing knowledge. Culturally it can be either very successful, or it can be a total failure. This will depend on the organisational culture influencing the knowledge management culture. If communities fail to be taken up into the organisation, individual ways of contributing to the knowledge management lifecycle should be created.

Training attendance

Training is an important way for staff members to acquire and share knowledge. Many organisations consider training to be very important and attendance is even measured on people's performance development programmes. Enquiries should be made either through a questionnaire or through interviews on whether staff members are attending the training that is allocated to them on an annual basis. It is very important to monitor training attendance, as this will indicate the growth in the organisation's knowledge base. If people tend to go on training enthusiastically, it indicates that the organisation has managed to develop a learning culture, which is very conducive to creating a knowledge management culture in the organisation.

If the knowledge management team picks up that staff members are not attending training that they are entitled to, it is indicative of a knowledge management lifecycle problem. The knowledge management team should then determine what the reasons behind this are. Examples could be that people are not given time by their superiors to attend the courses, or the money allocated to staff does not allow them to go to courses that would really build their skills base, or that certain staff members are deep specialists and e.g. need to go overseas to receive the training they need to advance their skills base. Once the knowledge management team understands what the issues are with respect to training problems, they should address this with Learning and Development or Human Resources in the organisation in order to rectify the issues where possible.

On the job training

It is important for the knowledge management team to understand how much on the job training takes place in the organisation's work environment. This will be a good indicator of the level of knowledge flow and knowledge sharing, especially between staff members on different hierarchical levels. The level of on the job training can be determined once again through interviews or questionnaires. If on the job training takes place regularly and well, it is an indicator that there is a natural flow of knowledge between different levels of people in the organisation in specific areas of specialisation. It is prudent for the knowledge management team to ask staff members why on the job training is working so well, to try and gain an insight into the organisation's knowledge management culture.

If on the job training does not take place regularly, it is not a good sign, as it shows that knowledge flow is stilted. Knowledge flow problems are not only taking place horizontally between colleagues, but also vertically in the hierarchy of that specific specialist area. The knowledge management team has to question the staff members as to why on the job training is not taking place and what they think would make it work effectively. The knowledge management team then needs to put remedial programmes in place to address these issues, as the knowledge management lifecycle becomes unbalanced if these activities are not addressed.

Values to be instilled to make knowledge management successful

The knowledge management team has to determine what values are to be instilled in the organisation to make knowledge management successful. This can also be determined by questionnaires or by interviews. Of all the questions asked to staff members, this is probably the most important question of all. Values play a very significant role in enabling the knowledge management lifecycle. Values such as trust, honesty, openness and transparency are invaluable to make a knowledge management programme successful. The emphasis on values will however, be different in different organisations, as organisational cultures differ.

It is important as well for the knowledge management team to understand what underlies the answers that the staff members give them, to have a more solid understanding of the knowledge management and organisational culture – whether it is good or bad, and whether it can be changed and if so, how.

This exercise is one of the most difficult exercises to execute, because people often struggle to bring personal values into context with knowledge sharing and the rest of the knowledge management lifecycle. It takes some time to think about how they tie together. Once they make the connection, however, they understand how fundamentally important it is to have the right value system before the organisation can have a successful knowledge management programme.

There is no real prescription on which values are more correct than others – it is dependent on each organisation to determine through the individuals that work there what the values are that they stand for and that they would like their knowledge management programme to be built upon.

The existence of informal mentoring relationships in the organisation

It is important to determine to what extent employees develop informal mentoring relationships with other staff members in the organisation. Mentorship is a facilitative way of sharing knowledge between people, usually of different levels in the hierarchy of an organisation. It is usually quite informal in nature and can be quite effective, as it can be a knowledge access point anywhere, anytime, any place.

Mentorship often not only assists with the sharing of knowledge, but can also lean towards the creation of knowledge, and one often finds that a staff member and a mentor can co-create knowledge on a specific topic. Mentoring thus draws on more than one aspect on the knowledge management lifecycle.

Mentoring is often tacit knowledge creation and sharing, rather than explicit in nature. The knowledge created can be very rewarding for the individuals concerned, but the value may be lost if not made explicit at some stage. That may make the process too rigid, however, which will make it lose some of its value. The right balance around this process needs to be found.

Locating experts in the organisation

Experts are often the gatekeepers to knowledge in the organisation. It is essential to know who they are to ensure that they can be utilised by the knowledge management programme. It is often difficult to determine who these gatekeepers of knowledge are. It can be done in a variety of ways, e.g. via interviews, questionnaires and through informal talking to staff members.

Once these gatekeepers or experts have been identified, a list of their names and the skills that they have must be drawn up and made available in the organisation in order for staff to be able to get to knowledge quicker and easier. The identification of these people is crucial to the success of the knowledge sharing network and it is important for the knowledge management programme manager to actively seek to identify these people.

Some organisations have skills databases where staff members can search their colleagues' skills and experience. This helps in finding the right person for the right piece of work. This increases the organisation's efficiency in deploying its human resources and building its knowledge and skills base.

Organisational and personal values

Is the practice of devoting time to knowledge creation encouraged, and if so, how?

Knowledge creation is as important in an organisation's knowledge management lifecycle as knowledge sharing. Often, knowledge management programmes just concentrate on knowledge sharing, whilst forgetting the innovation or knowledge creation part of the knowledge management lifecycle. It is important for the knowledge management department to determine if the organisation encourages workers to create new knowledge in their daily line of business, or to determine whether they mostly work with knowledge that already exists. It is also important to find out if they do devote time to knowledge creation, how they tend to it, as this will assist in further building on this knowledge management cultural activity.

The information that the knowledge management department will obtain from this investigation will yield a number of things. Firstly, it will tell a lot about the culture of the organisation. It will definitely expose if the organisation is an innovative organisation with creative minded employees or not. Secondly, it will show the knowledge management team whether the leadership team of the organisation places a premise on creating an innovative, open, thinking environment in place in the organisation. Once again, this will tell whether the organisation's culture is impacting on the knowledge management programme and culture. Finally, the information will inform the knowledge management team that there is or isn't a problem or an issue that needs attention in the creation area of the knowledge management lifecycle. If the team had detected issues, the reasons for the issues that they detected will help them to determine solutions to try and resolve this problem.

This is a very important issue in the knowledge management world, because if there is no creativity and innovation in an organisation there will be little growth in the knowledge base and it will become stale very quickly. Rejuvenation programmes will have to be implemented regularly to try and keep it fresh and in use by the staff members.

Is an organisational culture of 'knowledge is power' prevalent in the organisation, and if so, why?

The phenomenon of a culture of 'knowledge is power' in the organisation has to be investigated by the knowledge management team. The phenomenon can work in strange ways in organisations. Sometimes it is prevalent throughout the organisation. Sometimes it can be found in different departments of the organisation. Sometimes it is found within specific groups of people within departments.

Sometimes it is found that the phenomenon is found only *between* departments. And finally, sometimes, this phenomenon can also be found in individuals.

It is therefore very hard to firstly identify, and secondly, remedially address. The knowledge management team has to identify this as part of understanding both the organisational culture, as this also ties into values such as transparency, as well as knowledge management culture. It is once again also important to understand what the reasons are behind the culture of 'knowledge is power', as this will enable the knowledge management team later on to come up with workable solutions for particular environments.

The origins of 'knowledge is power' are based on the fact that knowledge is seen as a base of competitive advantage for an individual or a group of individuals. The knowledge management team should try and break down that perception and rather move to a perception where people who are sharing knowledge are publicly acknowledged, rewarded and seen as thought leaders in the organisation. This should be driven not only by the knowledge management team, but also by the organisational leadership team. In organisations where this model has been followed, knowledge management in all its lifecycle stages has been very successful. It is, however, not always easy to effect this change and it may take years to turn around the organisation and its staff members successfully (see Figure 14).

Do staff look to competitors, industry leaders and innovative organisations for the next generation of knowledge or procedures?

One of the next important questions that the knowledge management team should look at is whether employees look

Figure 14 The 'Knowledge is power' phenomenon

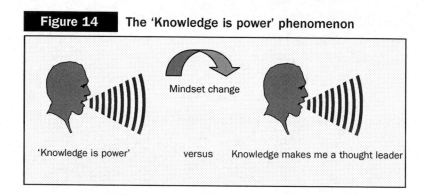

Mindset change

'Knowledge is power'   versus   Knowledge makes me a thought leader

to competitors, industry leaders and innovative organisations for the next generation of knowledge or procedures. Once again this is an important indicator of whether the organisation has a strong focus on the creation part of the knowledge management lifecycle. If they do tend to use others' work, there is nothing wrong with that – they are merely fulfilling the harvesting phase of the knowledge management lifecycle, which is also important. Yet the employees are not doing innovative, strategic thinking first, which shows that the culture of the organisation and of the knowledge management programme is not based on innovation and the creation of it's own knowledge.

Many organisations have found themselves in this situation before. Some organisations have consciously decided to get out of it by starting innovation programmes to encourage the creation of innovative ideas. The innovative ideas would then be furthered through a structured process until they are implemented, once selected as a good strategic or operational opportunity for somewhere in the organisation. Some organisations have even gone so far as to set up innovation incubators, where people are paid to come up with new ideas every day. Innovation as a discipline is also merging more and more with knowledge management as a discipline in the business world.

Measurement issues

Are the knowledge management lifecycle activities that staff participate in measured?

As discussed in previous chapters, reward and recognition for knowledge creation, sharing, harvesting and leveraging have been identified as being very valuable to staff members. The knowledge management team as well as the leadership team of the organisation is able to do this fairly easily on an ad hoc basis. To do this on a more structured basis, however, the activities that staff members participate in have to be measured. This means that the knowledge management programme manager and his or her team have to formulate, for different levels of staff in the organisations, specific measurements relating to knowledge management activities. These measures would, of course, be unique to each organisation. Examples of knowledge management measures are 'Are you seen by your peers as a thought leader in your specialist area', or 'How many contributions have you made to the communities of practice in your area of specialisation?'. Some measures the team may be able to quantify while others will be more qualitative in nature.

Once measurements are in place for different levels of staff, the measurements can be incorporated into the organisation's balanced score card, or performance appraisal system. Staff members will then regularly be measured on their behaviour with respect to the knowledge management lifecycle. This will provide much needed information for the knowledge management team on areas that need to be worked on and need attention, and they will be aware of areas where things are going well.

Based on the measurements, rewards and recognition can be given in a planned and structured way via the knowledge management programme to those who excelled.

Is knowledge creation and sharing recognised by the organisation, and if so, how?

The knowledge management team should inquire with staff members how they perceive the organisation to recognise knowledge creation and sharing. Once again it will provide the knowledge management team with invaluable information on how recognition takes place in the organisation and what the cultural issues around recognition are.

This provides the team with a platform to work from regarding recognition and reward issues. The information can be used to make positive changes and to ensure that recognition and reward definitely becomes an entrenched part of the knowledge management programme.

Is knowledge sharing rewarded by the organisation, and if so, how?

The knowledge management programme should determine whether staff are being rewarded by the organisation for knowledge sharing or not. Before that is done, the definition of 'reward' must be defined, because it can mean different things to different people. Reward can mean a monetary reward such as a bonus or a salary hike, or it could mean something like a prize such as a weekend away for two, or movie tickets, etc. Reward in some staff members' eyes can also equal recognition. The definition of reward will be unique in each organisation and hence it is important to define it properly up front.

Once defined, the knowledge management team should determine when people are rewarded, and if so, in what form. This is important to understand in order for the team to determine how to take the knowledge management programme forward with respect to mapping rewards to measurements and outcomes. If staff are not satisfied with the rewards that they receive, input should be obtained on what would be more appropriate to reward their knowledge sharing, and the knowledge management programme should be adapted accordingly if their suggestions are applicable and practical.

Rewards are very important on various levels as well, because staff share knowledge on various levels. Individuals share knowledge, so there should be rewards for individual knowledge sharing. Teams also share knowledge and should also be rewarded for team based knowledge sharing. This distinction is extremely important. If the organisation can master recognising and rewarding the individual contribution prior or before the team contribution, the phenomenon of 'knowledge is power' will be broken. At the end of the day, knowledge resides within the individual and this has to be recognised.

Are knowledge management lifecycle activities adequate? If not, what are the reasons and what can be done to rectify it?

The knowledge management team will also need to know whether knowledge management lifecycle activities are adequate, and if not, what the reasons are and what can be done to rectify it. It is important to have a balance across all activities of the knowledge management lifecycle, namely creation, sharing, harvesting, and leveraging of knowledge. It is therefore important to determine what activities are happening in each of the stages of the lifecycle. If these activities turn out to be inadequate, the knowledge management team needs to understand what the reasons are for the decline in certain issues in certain areas and what remedial actions can be taken to turn the situation around.

It will provide the knowledge management team with a good overall picture of the strong and weak points of their programme and where they need to focus in the near future. They may also hear from the staff members themselves possible solutions to rectify the issues that exist.

Strategy and leadership issues

Does the organisation's leadership team facilitate transparency on changes in the organisation?

The knowledge management team has to determine from staff members whether the management team facilitates transparency with respect to changes taking place in the organisation. Once again, this will provide the knowledge management team with a wealth of information on the culture of the organisation as well as the knowledge management behaviour in the organisation. If leaders create transparency in the face of change, it creates an open, honest, trusting environment where knowledge can be freely shared between people in all levels of the organisational hierarchy.

If the changes are not communicated by leadership, a climate of distrust is created and a lack of knowledge sharing is created, especially between levels of staff in the organisational hierarchy. Once again the organisational culture can be highly influential on the knowledge management culture and programme as a whole.

The knowledge management programme manager should coach leaders to understand the impact of how their leadership style impacts the organisation. They should be coached to do and say things in a way that will benefit the knowledge management programme going forward, in order for it not to be negatively impacted.

Do leaders allow staff members enough time to create and share knowledge?

Staff are often not allowed enough time to create and share knowledge during their daily work routine. Knowledge management staff have to enquire from them whether they are allowed to spend adequate time to create and share knowledge, or do they just get busy with their daily tasks and end up not getting to knowledge management activities. If they are not allowed to get to knowledge management activities or are impeded to do so (e.g. by a time billing system where time booked on actual work is rewarded and knowledge management activities are not), the knowledge management programme needs to revisit the recognition and reward programme in the organisation, as people should have time to spend on these knowledge management activities.

If it is a case that people get tied up with their normal daily work, then it signals that they still do not perceive knowledge management as being crucial to the success of the organisation and culturally knowledge management has not been taken up. A cultural solution should then be put into place to change mindsets of staff to ensure that they see knowledge management activities as just as important as their other daily work activities.

Process issues

Do formal organisational processes exist to share knowledge?

The knowledge management team must determine whether any formal knowledge sharing or any other formal knowledge management process exist in the organisation. Processes play a very important role in embedding knowledge into the organisation, as knowledge always flows within a process. If any formal knowledge sharing or knowledge management processes exist, they need to be formally mapped. An ideal value chain of knowledge management processes must then be identified and the gaps identified. The gaps must be filled by drawing the future state maps and enhancing the current processes. This will provide the organisation with the ideal processes for the future knowledge management programme. These must then be implemented through an organisation wide training programme where staff are trained on how the processes work and what they aim to achieve.

Do mechanisms exist to facilitate feedback from work that has been completed in order to facilitate lessons learned?

Lessons learned are a very powerful way to share knowledge amongst staff members. The knowledge management team must identify whether the organisation have a mechanism by which they facilitate feedback from work that has been completed in order to facilitate lessons learned. If the organisation has such a mechanism, the levels of usage need to be determined. If low, then the knowledge management team needs to understand the reasons for the usage being so low and how this can be fixed.

If the organisation has no such facility, the knowledge management team should organise co-creation sessions with stakeholders from areas throughout the business and design a lessons learned feedback mechanism that will work in their particular environments. It should be something that they feel they own and would like to participate in and learn from.

Most organisations express a need for a mechanism of this nature, albeit in various shapes and forms. Everyone acknowledges that there is a lot to learn from past successes, but also from past failures.

Are there any measures in place to translate tacit knowledge to explicit knowledge, and if so, what are they?

Translating tacit knowledge to explicit knowledge is one of the most difficult knowledge management tasks, but probably one of the most valuable ones if it can be done. Due to the fact that it is such a valuable task, it is important for the knowledge management team to determine whether the organisation has any measures in place to translate tacit knowledge to explicit knowledge. Although it is impossible to translate all of a person's tacit knowledge to explicit format, some portion of it can made explicit.

If there are measures in place, the knowledge management team need to understand whether these measures are working or not, and if not, what the reasons for that are and how staff think it can be resolved. If there are no measures, the knowledge management team needs to put measures in place to translate tacit knowledge to an explicit format. This is not an easy task, and the measures will be unique to every organisation, but they are extremely important. This must be one of the things that staff members must be measured on to ensure that the organisation's attrition rate does not have such a huge impact on the organisation (see Figure 15).

Figure 15	Translating tacit knowledge to explicit knowledge is extremely valuable to the organisation

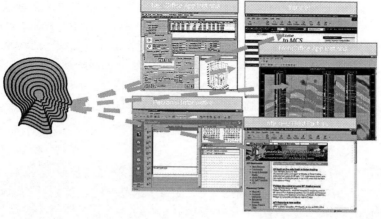

Technology and other channel issues

Do any reporting mechanisms exist to report information that may be useful in the future?

The knowledge management team needs to determine whether any reporting mechanisms exist to report any information that may be useful in the future, e.g. models, methodologies and templates. This is important to ensure that knowledge in the organisation is not re-used, but can be saved in a central repository in order for it to be available to all in the organisation. It can then be re-used in its original format, or changed to suit the context it is needed in.

The knowledge management team needs to determine how this process will work. It is one of the most difficult processes in the knowledge management processes, as it is difficult to identify firstly what a re-usable piece of information is, secondly who the responsible parties are that should identify them and archive them centrally, and further what the feedback mechanisms look like.

There are various options to choose from. The knowledge management team can do it in a manual way with teams on a regular basis, identifying certain reusable, generic material that should be kept for re-use. The alternative is that gatekeepers or thought leaders should be identified and that this should be one of their performance measurements to identify generic material that should be uploaded on to the knowledge management system for re-use in other contexts. The other option is just to keep it open and let anyone upload material as they see fit. The danger in this option is that it most often does not happen, and valuable knowledge does not filter through to the rest of the organisation for re-use.

How would you rate the ease of access to knowledge pertaining to work or customers?

The knowledge management team should assess from staff members the ease of access to knowledge in the organisation. This refers specifically to the ease of access through technology. This is an important question to ask, as most organisations have technology available where information and knowledge can and are being stored on.

The knowledge management team will typically find two scenarios. The first scenario will be that there is a lack of ease of access as the information and knowledge is not stored on technology based systems at all. The second scenario could be that there is a lack of ease of access due to the fact that the technology systems do not exist to store the knowledge and information on. The third scenario is that staff members often work remotely and cannot get remote access to their organisational knowledge bases, intranet, etc., or if they can, it is very slow and basically unusable. The fourth scenario could be that people are not trained to use the technology to extract the knowledge and information that they need from the technology based systems that are available to them.

The knowledge management team may find any of the scenarios when they interview staff members and they may even find additional scenarios and issues. It may very well differ from organisation to organisation. It is, however, important to understand what technology issues are hampering the knowledge management lifecycle, because, although knowledge management is not only based on technology, technology is an important component of knowledge management.

Once the knowledge management team understands what the issues are with respect to the ease of access to knowledge and information in technology based systems in the organisations, they can go ahead and start designing new solutions to resolve the issues at hand. Often this is an iterative processes, because the uptake of technology and associated processes and solutions are also closely tied to organisational and knowledge management culture.

Is technology a barrier to knowledge access and if so, why?

Technology can be a big barrier to an organisation's success for many reasons, e.g. if people are not properly trained to use the technology, if they cannot apply the technology to resolve certain problems, or if technology has not been implemented correctly and is down or provides issues or operational problems.

The knowledge management team needs to determine whether technology is seen as a barrier to knowledge access, and if so why. It is very important to understand this, as technology can really hamper the access to knowledge. The reasons staff members give for technology being a barrier to knowledge access can indicate to the team what the underlying issues and problems are, in order for them to focus on where they should spend their time on creating solutions for the problems.

In many instances, it is simply a matter of user training that is lacking. People do not understand how to use knowledge management systems and therefore do not have access to the knowledge they need. Another problem is often operational issues, e.g. systems that are very slow, or that can't be accessed remotely.

The knowledge management team needs to find workarounds for these problems if possible to make it easy for users to access organisational knowledge.

Organisational structure issues

Does silo knowledge sharing behaviour exist in the organisation and if so to what extent and why?

Silo knowledge sharing and creating behaviour often exists in organisations. This often happens in different departments of the organisations, or in different specialisation areas of the organisation. Knowledge flow is hampered by this silo behaviour. The knowledge management team should determine if silo knowledge management behaviour exists in the organisation, and if so to what extent and what the reasons are behind the silo behaviour.

If the silo behaviour is found to be a huge problem, the knowledge management team should look at the business process value chain and how knowledge and information flows through it in order to determine where the bottlenecks are. The knowledge management team also needs to determine why these bottlenecks happen and what the exact reasons are for the silo behaviour. This is extremely important to enable the knowledge management team to build programmes to entrench a culture of integration and embedding of knowledge in the organisational value chain, which will minimise silo behaviour.

How well does knowledge transfer take place between staff levels with varying levels of expertise and experience? If it does not take place well, what are the potential reasons?

Organisational hierarchy can have huge impact on the flow of knowledge in an organisation. Often, the more levels in the organisation's hierarchy, the less knowledge are shared. The flatter the organisational hierarchy, the more transparent the organisation is and the more knowledge are

Figure 16   Translating tacit knowledge to explicit knowledge between different levels of staff is extremely valuable to the organisation

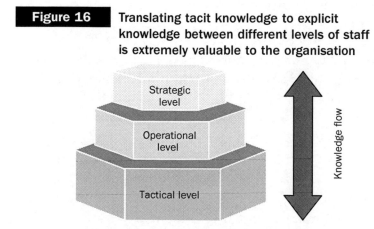

shared. Knowledge is shared more easily both on a horizontal and vertical level.

The knowledge management team should determine how well knowledge transfer takes place between staff levels with varying levels of expertise and experience. If it does not take place well, they should determine what the potential reasons are. Once they understand the potential reasons, it is easier to come up with potential solutions to get the knowledge sharing and knowledge flow going. These reasons may be unique in each organisation, so there is no real blueprint to deal with these issues and there are also no standard solutions. Solutions have to be built on a one-on-one basis (see Figure 16).

6

Conclusions

Every organisation has an absolutely unique organisational culture made up by the values that its staff members bring to their daily place of work. This organisational culture determines how people act, how work is executed, and how human interaction takes place. It dictates how the organisation operates from day to day.

In the knowledge management environment, in many cases however, little attention is often paid to organisational culture, whilst it is such a pervasive force in the knowledge management world. A lot of attention is paid to technology – to intranets and databases and search engines and tools to make the knowledge management lifecycle faster and more efficient. Knowledge management programmes also focus on processes and on how the knowledge management lifecycle should be executed. Processes are mapped and followed. Yet these organisations still find that their knowledge management programmes are not functioning optimally. This is because they are not dealing with the cultural issues in the organisation and within the knowledge management programme itself. Sometimes this is done deliberately, because it is one of the hardest tasks to undertake. Sometimes it is not undertaken out of ignorance of the huge impact that it has on the organisation.

Organisations need to take note of the impact of organisational culture on knowledge management when they embark on a knowledge management implementation. They should take every detail of the organisational culture into consideration when designing the knowledge management programme. Once the knowledge management programme has been implemented, the knowledge management team should ensure that the impact of the organisational culture on the knowledge management programme is identified and managed, or else the knowledge management programme will never really be successful.

'Dipstick' surveys of the state of the organisational culture should be undertaken on a regular basis, as organisational culture can also change over time. It can also change if there is a special event, e.g. a merger or acquisition. These dipsticks will provide valuable information to the knowledge management programme management team to adapt the knowledge management programme to fit in with the organisational culture, which will address the resistance to new programmes such as knowledge management.

Knowledge and how it is made up as part of the human psyche is not yet fully understood. Managing it as an individual's asset and an organisation's resource remains one of the biggest challenges of our time. It is important for us as humans, to never forget the human element of knowledge when we talk about the science of knowledge management. Knowledge originated from humans and is managed by humans and therefore we can never forget the human dynamics when we look toward implementing a programme as complex as a knowledge management programme. If we do, we will fail miserably, and become a group of technology based robots with no innovation capacity. The era of knowledge and knowledge management will end and the human race will all be the poorer for it.

References

Chait, L.P. (1999) 'Creating a successful knowledge management system', *Journal of Business Strategy*, March–April; available at: *http://web7.infotrac.london. galegroup.com/itw/infomark/482/356/72858976w3/ purl=rc1_GBIM_0_A54293715&dyn=26!xrn_1_0_ A54293715?sw_aep=up_itw*

Darling, M.S. (2000) 'Building the knowledge organisation', *Business Quarterly*, 61(2): 61–7; available at: *http://web4. infotrac.london.galegroup.com/itw/infomark/611/543/ 72569684w3/purl=rc2_GBIM_1_Michele+S.+Darling_ 1996_Business+Quarterly_&dyn=sig!11?sw_aep=up_itw*

Davenport, T. (1999) 'Knowledge management, round two', *CIO Magazine*, Nov. 1; available at: *http://www.cio.com/ archive/110199_think_content.html*

Du Plessis, M. and Boon J.A. (2004) 'The role of knowledge management in eBusiness and customer relationship management: South African case study findings', *International Journal of Information Management*, 24(1): 73–86.

Du Plessis, M. (2005) 'Drivers of knowledge management in the corporate environment', *International Journal of Information Management*, 25(3): 193–202.

Du Plessis, M. (2003) 'The role of knowledge management in eBusiness and customer relationship management'. PhD Thesis, University of Pretoria, Pretoria, South Africa.

Gartner Ggroup (2000) 'KM benefits: from building productivity to creating wealth', Gartner Group report, Apr; available at: *http://gartner4/gartnerweb.com:80/ glet/purchase/g/lc/is0/4010/001/doc/glcis04010001/*

Gordon, J.H. and Smith, C. (2006) *Applied knowledge and innovation: knowledge management guidelines.* Available at: *http://www.akri.org/research/km.htm*

Greco, J. (1999) 'Knowledge is power', *Journal of Business Strategy*, March–April; available at: *http://web7.infotrac. london.galegroup.com/itw/infomark/482/356/ 72858976w3/purl=rc1_GBIM_0_A54293713&dyn= 30!xrn_10_0_A54293713?sw_aep=up_itw*

Hall, H. (2006) 'KM, culture and compromise: devising practical interventions to promote knowledge sharing in corporate environments'. Available at: *http://www.dcs. napier.asw/n/hazelh/esis/hall_ebic_os.pdf*

Hargadon, A. and Sutton, R.I. (2000) 'Building an innovation factory', *Harvard Business Review*, 78(3): 157–66; available at: *http://proquest.umi.com/pqdweb*

Havens, C. and Knapp, E. (1999) 'Easing into knowledge management', *Strategy & Leadership*, 27(2): 4–10; available at: *http://web4.infotrac.london.galegroup.com/ itw/infomark/430/644/72715798w3/purl=rc1_GBIM_0_ A54370966&dyn=16!bmk_1_0_A54370966?sw_aep= up_itw*

Hickins, M. (1999) 'Xerox shares its knowledge', *Management Review*, Sept. 1999: 40; available at: *http://web2.infotrac.london.galegroup.com/itw/infomark/ 740/622/72562376w3/purl=rc1_GBIM_0_A55676727& dyn=3!xrn_5_0_A55676727?sw_aep=up_itw*

Kennedy, M.L. (1996) 'Positioning strategic information: partnering for the information advantage', *Special Libraries*, 87(2): 120–32; available at: *http://web4. infotrac.london.galegroup.com/itw/infomark/430/644/*

72715798w3/purl=rc2_GBIM_2_mary+lee+kennedy_1996_&dyn=sig!28?sw_aep=up_itw

KPMG Consulting (2000) *Knowledge management research report 2000*. Available at: *http://www.kpmgconsulting.com* (accessed 26/09/2000).

Merali, Y. (2000) 'Self-organising communities'. In *Liberating Knowledge* (Reeves, J., Ed.). London: Caspian Publishing, pp. 80–7.

Mudge, A. (1999) 'Knowledge management: do we know what we know?', *Communication World*, 16(5): 24–9; available at: *http://web4.infotrac.london.galegroup.com/itw/infomark/430/644/72715798w3/purl=rc2_GBIM_2_alden+mudge_1999_&dyn=sig!29?sw_aep=up_itw*

Nichani, M. (2004) *Understanding organisational culture for knowledge sharing*. Available at: *http://community. flexiblelearning.net.au/GlobalPerspectives/content/article_6193.htm* (accessed 12/06/2006).

O'Dell, C. and Grayson, C.J. Jr. (1999) 'Knowledge transfer: discover your value proposition', *Strategy & Leadership*, 27(2): 10–6; available at: *http://web4.infotrac.london. galegroup.com/itw/infomark/430/644/72715798w3/ purl=rc2_GBIM_2_knowledge+transfer_1999_Strategy+ %26+Leadership_&dyn=sig!22?sw_aep=up_itw*

Parlby, D. and Taylor, R. (2000) *The power of knowledge: a business guide to knowledge management*. Available at: *http://www.kpmgconsulting.com/index.html* (accessed 31/10/2000).

PriceWaterhouseCoopers (1999) Inside the mind of the CEO: the 1999 global CEO survey. *World Economic Forum*, 1999 Annual Meeting, Davos, Switzerland. Available at: *http://www.pwcglobal.com/extweb/ncsurvres.nsf/DocID/ BA7779AD2FBCB621852568DA00311F64* (accessed 05/10/2000).

Reiss, D.A. (1999) 'Companies need to learn how to leverage knowledge to sustain competitive advantage'. Available at: *http://www.ey.com/global/gcr.nsf/US/ Knowledge_- _Real_Estate_-_Ernst_&_Young_LLP*

Snowden, D. (2000) 'Liberating knowledge'. In *Liberating knowledge* (Reeves, J., Ed.). London: Caspian Publishing, pp. 6–19.

Stahle, P. (2000) 'New challenges of knowledge management'. In *Liberating knowledge* (Reeves, J., Ed.). London: Caspian Publishing, pp. 36–42.

Temkin, L. (2001) 'Building tomorrow's corporate portal'. In *Infosmart Africa 2001. 10–12 July 2001 Conference Proceedings*, Gauteng, South Africa. Johannesburg: Terrapin.

Van Der Kamp, M. (2001) 'A corporate portal for customer intelligence'. In *Infosmart Africa 2001. 10–12 July 2001 Conference Proceedings*, Gauteng, South Africa. Johannesburg: Terrapin.

Van Der Spek, R. and Kingma, J. (2000) 'Achieving successful knowledge management initiatives'. In *Liberating knowledge* (Reeves, J., Ed.). London: Caspian Publishing, pp. 20–30.

Vernon, M. (1999) '"Knowledge paradox" puts Europe ahead: Europe versus the US', *Financial Times*, Nov. 10: 11. Available at: *http://web4.infotrac.london.galegroup. com/itw/infomark/430/644/72715798w3/purl=rc1_GBI M_0_CJ57472030&dyn=71!xrn_1_0_CJ57472030?sw_ aep=up_itw*

Zyngier, S.M. (2006) *Knowledge management obstacles in Australia.* Available at: *http://64.233.183.104.search? q=cache:4141oqWR23EJ:is2.1se.ac.uk/asp/asp/aspecis/ 20020142.pdf+km+organisational+culture&hl=en&gl=u*

Index